EVERYONE**CAN**COOK

over 120 recipes for entertaining everyday

ERIC AKIS

EVERYONE**CAN**COOK

over 120 recipes for entertaining everyday

whitecap

Edited by Elaine Jones
Proofread by Marial Shea
Cover and interior design by Jacqui Thomas
Food photographs by Michael Tourigny
Food styling by Eric Akis

PRINTED AND BOUND IN CANADA

National Library of Canada Cataloguing in Publication Data

Akis, Eric, 1961-
  Everyone can cook / Eric Akis.

  ISBN 1-55285-448-5

  1. Quick and easy cookery.   I. Title.
TX833.5.A34 2003   641.5'55   C2003-910252-1

The publisher acknowledges the support of the Canada Council for the Arts and the Cultural Services Branch of the Government of British Columbia for our publishing program. We acknowledge the financial support of the Government of Canada through the Book Publishing Industry Development Program for our publishing activities.

EVERYONE CANCOOK

CONTENTS

Dedication	VI
Acknowledgements	VI
Introduction	VII
Fabulous Finger Foods	1
Sumptuous Salads	17
Seasonal Soups	31
Using Your Noodles	45
Simply Seafood	59
Vegetarian Entrées	79
Chicken and Other Fine-Tasting Fowl	91
Meaty Mains	113
On the Side	139
A Jar Full of Cookies	153
Divine Desserts	167
Index	180

DEDICATION

To my late father, Imants (Bill) Akis, and my dear mother, Julie Akis, without whose love and support and willingness to sample my creations when I was just a boy, my culinary career and this book would have never become a reality. And to Sandy Wong, my first and greatest mentor, who encouraged me to sample, explore and never stop learning about the wonderful world of food. Finally, to my wife, Cheryl, and son, Tyler. Your love, your caring and your appetite for fine food made creating the recipes for this book a taste-filled adventure.

ACKNOWLEDGEMENTS

I've been overwhelmed and so grateful for the amazing support I've received during the creation of this book—a process that started years before the first page was typed.

I want to give a special thank you to Carolyn Heiman, features editor of the *Victoria Times-Colonist*, who hired me, a chef with no formal writing experience, over several other professional writers as her food writer in 1997. If not for her I would not have the tools I needed to write this book. The job gave me the chance to thoroughly explore the world of food, establish myself as a food authority and build an audience for my columns and recipes, not only in Victoria but also in cities across Canada. It also opened up other career opportunities.

The most important was when Alex Campbell Junior of Thrifty Foods hired me to create recipes for his company. I want to thank Alex again for that opportunity, as it brought me in close contact with food shoppers and opened my eyes to what home cooks are looking for in a recipe.

These two developments in my culinary career built the foundation for my next step: a cookbook proposal to Whitecap Books. Thank you to Whitecap for so readily accepting my idea. Thanks to Leanne, Robin, Sophie, Claire, Christine, Roberta, Aydin, Marial and Jacqui at Whitecap for so efficiently guiding me through the many steps required to publish and launch a cookbook.

Beyond the capable folks at Whitecap, I would also like to acknowledge the tremendous help Patrick Derricourt, Alison Field, Liz Pogue, Ralf Mundel and Arthur Gilligan contributed to this project. Thanks to Michael Tourigny and his assistant Michelle Yee for taking the wonderful photographs in the book and—equally as important—for their friendship and their belief in my goals and dreams. And thank you to Elaine Jones for so skilfully editing this book.

Finally, thanks to all the people who have tried my recipes and taken the time to chat or send notes to say how much you enjoyed them. Your words of encouragement keep me headed to the kitchen day after day, creating tasty recipes that everyone can cook.

INTRODUCTION

Over the past few years I have created hundreds of recipes for my weekly columns in the *Victoria Times-Colonist* and for Thrifty Foods, a forward-thinking supermarket chain that hired me to create four recipes each week from items featured in their flyer. Through countless one-on-one conversations with readers and shoppers, I've developed a keen sense of what home cooks are looking for: recipes that everyone — not just five-star chefs — can cook.

First, and not surprisingly, people want recipes that are easy to follow and use easily accessible ingredients. They should, when possible, offer some flexibility too. This might include suggestions for substitutions or omitting certain ingredients that might not appeal to everyone.

Home cooks want recipes that will allow them to quickly create a dish with flavour and flair. And sometimes they look for recipes that challenge, but don't intimidate. They may decide to take the time to create wonderful soups, dinners or desserts even if it occupies a whole Sunday afternoon, but they also need to be assured that the result will be worth it.

I've taken all these comments to heart and incorporated them into my recipes. The feedback has been very positive; readers have told me that my recipes make them look like superstars when they host a party, but it is all so very easy.

In response to my readers, I have put together a collection of the most requested recipes in this cookbook. You'll find a wide selection of inviting dishes that follow the guidelines outlined above. Some dishes are designed for everyday cooking, others for special occasions. The majority of them offer options for tweaking the recipe to make it more to your liking, widen its use, or heighten its flavour even more. Feel free to dive in and make your own changes, such as substituting pecans for walnuts, using tender young salad greens instead of spinach, or adding a favourite spice or herb to give a dish an extra zing.

Everyone Can Cook is meant to sit on a kitchen shelf, not the coffee table. My goal is that, like other frequently used cookbooks, the pages will become dog-eared and stained over the years. Enjoy!

Port-Marinated Strawberries   2
Wrapped in Prosciutto

Tortilla Chips with Shrimp   3
and Corn Salsa

Zucchini Rounds with Cambozola   4
and Cherry Tomatoes

Greek-Style Mini Burgers   5
on Cucumber Rounds

Chicken Wings with   6
Heat, Honey and Rum

Japanese-Style Chicken   7
Skewers with Ginger Sauce

Hot-Smoked Salmon   8
on Mini New Potatoes

FABULOUS FINGER FOODS

CHAPTER ONE

New York Steak Crostini   9
with Gremolata Mayonnaise

Brandy-Laced Peppercorn   10
Pâté on Baguette Rounds

Roasted Pepper Antipasto   12
on Parmesan Toasts

Pork and Crab   14
Pot Stickers

Caramelized Onion   16
and Stilton Tarts

PORT-MARINATED STRAWBERRIES WRAPPED IN PROSCIUTTO

preparation time · 20 minutes
cooking time · none
makes · 24 pieces

These little bites offer an intriguing blend of sweet, salty and tangy. I like to serve them at an alfresco summer gathering when strawberries are in season.

ERIC'S OPTIONS
Use fresh figs, halved, or small slices of honeydew or cantaloupe melon instead of strawberries. You could also use a combination of fruits.

12	large strawberries, halved	12
1/4 cup	port	50 mL
to taste	freshly cracked black pepper	to taste
3/4 cup	goat cheese	175 mL
12	paper-thin slices prosciutto, each cut in half	12

Place the strawberries in a single layer on a plate. Drizzle with port and sprinkle with black pepper. Cover with plastic wrap and let stand for 30 minutes at room temperature.

Place a small spoonful of goat cheese on the cut side of each strawberry. Wrap each strawberry with a half-slice of prosciutto. Arrange on a decorative platter and serve.

HOW TO BUY PROSCIUTTO
This salt-cured, air-dried Italian-style ham is expensive, but a little goes a long way. When you buy it, ask for it to be sliced paper-thin. If necessary, ask your retailer to trim away the tough outer rind before it's sliced. When it's packaged ask them to put a layer of paper between each slice. If the slices overlap, they will stick together and be very difficult to pull apart.

TORTILLA CHIPS with SHRIMP and CORN SALSA

preparation time · 15 minutes
cooking time · none
makes · 24 pieces

These quick-to-make appetizers are a tasty, fun and colourful item to serve a gathering of friends. Use store-bought salsa or make Speedy Salsa (page 142).

ERIC'S OPTIONS
Thin slices of grilled chicken breast or tender beef steak could replace the shrimp.

1/4 cup	fresh cooked or frozen (thawed) corn kernels	50 mL
1/3 cup	salsa	75 mL
24	large tortilla chips	24
1/4 cup	sour cream	50 mL
3/4 lb.	cooked salad shrimp	375 g
	fresh cilantro sprigs or sliced green onion for garnish	

Combine the corn and salsa. Top each tortilla chip, as close to serving time as possible to keep the chips crisp, with a small spoonful of the sour cream. Top the sour cream with a small spoonful of salsa. Arrange a few shrimp on top of the salsa and garnish with a small sprig of cilantro or slice of green onion. Serve immediately.

PLANNING AN APPETIZER MENU

The time and length of your event will determine what type of appetizers you make and how many. Before a multi-course lunch or dinner, allow an appetite-awakening, but not filling, 2–3 pieces per person. For gatherings in mid-afternoon or early evening, a few hours after lunch or a few hours before dinner, allow 4–6 pieces per person. For longer evening events, where the finger food will substitute for dinner, allow a meal-sized 8–10 pieces per person. Use a balanced approached when choosing what to serve and offer vegetarian, seafood and meat items, serving some hot and some cold.

ZUCCHINI ROUNDS with CAMBOZOLA and CHERRY TOMATOES

preparation time · 20 minutes
cooking time · 10–12 minutes
makes · 24 pieces

These tiny pizza-like rounds offer an enticing, meatless way to awaken your taste buds.

ERIC'S OPTIONS
Use similar-sized yellow zucchini, sometimes called summer squash, to replace the common variety. For a really colourful presentation, use a combination of both when available.

2	medium zucchini, each cut into 12 rounds 1/2 inch (1 cm) thick	2
3 1/2 oz.	Cambozola cheese	100 g
6	large cherry tomatoes, each cut into 4 slices	6
	extra virgin olive oil	
to taste	salt and freshly cracked black pepper	to taste
	fresh basil, parsley or oregano leaves for garnish	

Preheat the oven to 350°F (180°C). Scoop out a little from the centre of each zucchini round and place the rounds scooped side up on a baking tray. Fill the centres with a small nugget of Cambozola cheese. Top with a tomato slice. Drizzle with a little olive oil and season with salt and pepper. Bake for 10–12 minutes. Cool slightly before arranging on a serving tray. Garnish each zucchini round with an herb sprig and serve.

GREEK-STYLE MINI BURGERS on CUCUMBER ROUNDS

preparation time ·	20 minutes	
cooking time ·	4–6 minutes	
makes ·	12–14 pieces	

Cucumber rounds provide a low-calorie base for these tasty morsels. Use store-bought or your own Tzatziki (page 144).

ERIC'S OPTIONS
Substitute similar-sized slices of zucchini for the cucumber. Brush them with olive oil, grill until firm-tender and cool to room temperature before topping.

1/2 lb.	ground lamb or beef	250 g
1	large egg	1
1 Tbsp.	chopped fresh mint	15 mL
1 Tbsp.	chopped fresh oregano	15 mL
2	garlic cloves, chopped	2
1/4 cup	bread crumbs	50 mL
1 Tbsp.	lemon juice	15 mL
to taste	salt and freshly cracked black pepper	to taste
1/2 cup	tzatziki	125 mL
12–14	slices English cucumber, cut 1/4 inch (5 mm) thick	12–14
	small sprigs mint or oregano and olive slices for garnish	

Combine the meat with the egg, mint, oregano, garlic, bread crumbs, lemon juice, salt and pepper. Mix well. Form into small patties about 2 inches (5 cm) wide and 1/4 inch (5 mm) thick. Pan-fry, broil or grill the patties until cooked through, about 2–3 minutes per side. (Patties can be cooked ahead, cooled, stored in the fridge and reheated when needed.) Spoon a little tzatziki on each slice of cucumber and place a burger on top. Top with a little more tzatziki sauce and garnish with a mint or oregano sprig and an olive slice.

CHICKEN WINGS with HEAT, HONEY and RUM

preparation time	·	10 minutes
cooking time	·	25–30 minutes
makes	·	24 pieces

There's a taste of the Caribbean in these easy-to-make wings. They are a great snack when the big game's on.

ERIC'S OPTIONS
For a spicier, even more Caribbean-like taste, add a pinch of clove and nutmeg to the marinade before adding the wings. This marinade will also work for 24 raw, boneless chicken breast strips. Marinate the strips as described, threading on skewers and grilling.

1/4 cup	liquid honey	50 mL
1/4 cup	dark rum	50 mL
to taste	your favourite hot sauce (be bold)	to taste
2	limes, juiced	2
2	garlic cloves, chopped	2
1 tsp.	grated fresh ginger	5 mL
24	chicken wingettes or drumettes, or a mix of both	24
to taste	salt	to taste

Combine the honey, rum, hot sauce, lime juice, garlic and ginger in a bowl. Add the wings and toss to coat completely. Marinate for 2–3 hours in the refrigerator.

Preheat the oven to 425°F (220°C). Place the wings in a single layer on a baking sheet. Pour the marinade over them. Sprinkle with salt. Bake for 25–30 minutes, or until cooked through. Place the wings on a serving tray and spoon pan juices over them.

JAPANESE-STYLE CHICKEN SKEWERS with GINGER SAUCE

preparation time ·	25 minutes	
cooking time ·	15–20 minutes	
makes ·	24 skewers	

Baking these skewers, rather than grilling or broiling them, makes them much easier to cook — the wooden skewers are less prone to burning in the oven, and no flipping is required.

NOTE
Teriyaki sauce is sold in the Asian food aisle of most supermarkets.

ERIC'S OPTIONS
You can use tender beef, pork or turkey strips instead of chicken. For beef, reduce the cooking time to about 10 minutes for medium-rare meat.

1 1/4 lb.	boneless skinless chicken breast	625 g
1 cup	teriyaki sauce	250 mL
24	wooden skewers	24
3/4 cup	mayonnaise	175 mL
1 Tbsp.	grated or finely chopped fresh ginger	15 mL
2 Tbsp.	sesame seeds	25 mL
1/4 cup	chopped fresh cilantro or green onions	50 mL

Cut the chicken into 24 thin strips and place in a bowl. Pour in 3/4 cup (175 mL) of the teriyaki sauce and gently toss. Cover and marinate in the fridge for several hours, or over-night. Prepare 24 wooden skewers by soaking them in cold water for at least 1 hour while the chicken marinates. To make the sauce, combine the remaining 1/4 cup (50 mL) of teriyaki sauce with the mayonnaise and ginger in a small bowl. Cover with plastic wrap and store in the fridge until needed.

Preheat the oven to 450°F (230°C). Thread the chicken onto the skewers. Place skewers in a single layer on a large, non-stick or parchment-lined baking tray. Brush with the marinade and sprinkle with sesame seeds. Bake for 15–20 minutes, or until cooked through. Arrange on a serving tray and brush with the pan juices. Sprinkle with cilantro or green onions. Serve the sauce alongside for dipping.

HOT-SMOKED SALMON
on MINI NEW POTATOES

preparation time · 20 minutes
cooking time · 15 minutes
makes · 24 pieces

Hot-smoked salmon is less expensive than cold-smoked salmon or lox, but it can be equally delicious. It's sold in small pieces at most seafood counters.

ERIC'S OPTIONS
For a richer version of this dish, top the salmon with a small spoon of caviar before garnishing with dill. Other seafood, such as crabmeat, thinly sliced lobster meat or salad shrimp, can replace the smoked salmon.

12	mini red or white new potatoes	12
1/2 cup	sour cream	125 mL
2 tsp.	chopped fresh dill	10 mL
to taste	salt, pepper, lemon juice and horseradish	to taste
3/4 lb.	hot-smoked salmon, skin removed, flaked into pieces	375 g
24	small dill sprigs	24

Cut the potatoes in half. Trim a little from the uncut side so they will sit flat. Boil the potatoes in lightly salted water until just tender. Drain well and cool to room temperature. Set on a serving tray cut side up. In a small bowl combine the sour cream and chopped dill. Season with salt, pepper, lemon juice and horseradish. Spoon a small amount of this mixture on top of each potato. Top with a piece or two of flaked salmon. Garnish with a dill sprig and serve.

NEW YORK STEAK CROSTINI
with GREMOLATA MAYONNAISE

preparation time	·	25 minutes
cooking time	·	15–20 minutes
makes	·	24 pieces

Include these hearty, more filling bites when you are making a meal of appetizers.

ERIC'S OPTIONS
Top sirloin, rib-eye and tenderloin steaks are other cuts of beef that could be used in this recipe.

1 1/2 lbs.	New York steak	750 g
	olive oil	
to taste	salt and freshly cracked black pepper	to taste
24	thin baguette rounds	24
1/4 cup	freshly grated Parmesan cheese	50 mL
1/2 cup	mayonnaise	125 mL
2 Tbsp.	chopped fresh parsley	25 mL
2 tsp.	finely grated lemon zest	10 mL
2	garlic cloves, crushed	2
to taste	salt, freshly cracked black pepper and lemon juice	to taste
24	sprigs Italian parsley	24

Brush the steak with a little olive oil and season generously with salt and pepper. Grill, broil or pan-fry the steak to the desired doneness. Allow the meat to rest for 10 minutes to allow the juices to set before thinly slicing it.

Meanwhile, brush the baguette rounds lightly with olive oil and place them in a single layer on a baking tray. Sprinkle the tops with cheese. Broil until lightly toasted, then set aside until cool enough to handle.

Combine the mayonnaise, chopped parsley, lemon zest and garlic in a bowl. Season with salt, pepper and lemon juice. Place a spoon of mayonnaise on each baguette round, reserving about half the mayonnaise for the tops. Top with 2–3 slices of the steak, dividing the meat evenly between the rounds. Top the steak with a spoon of the remaining mayonnaise. Garnish with a sprig of parsley. Serve immediately.

BRANDY-LACED PEPPERCORN PÂTÉ on BAGUETTE ROUNDS

preparation time · 15 minutes
cooking time · 12–15 minutes
makes · about 2 cups (500 mL) pâté

This divine pâté freezes well when sealed in an airtight container. Thaw it in the fridge overnight before using.

1/2 lb.	butter, at room temperature	250 g
1	medium onion, halved and thinly sliced	1
3	garlic cloves, chopped	3
1 lb.	chicken livers, trimmed of fat and sinew	500 g
1/2 tsp.	dried thyme	2 mL
2 Tbsp.	green peppercorns	25 mL
1/4 cup	brandy	50 mL
to taste	salt and freshly cracked black pepper	to taste
24–30	lightly toasted baguette rounds	24–30
	thinly sliced gherkins and parsley sprigs for garnish	

Melt 3 Tbsp. (45 mL) of the butter in a skillet set over medium heat. Add the onion and garlic and cook until tender. Add the chicken livers and thyme and cook until the livers are nicely coloured and almost cooked through. (Cut a chicken liver open during cooking to see how they are doing. They should look just slightly pink in the middle. Be careful not to overcook them or the pâté will have a less-appealing look, colour and taste.) Add the green peppercorns and brandy. If desired, carefully ignite it with a long match. Cook, stirring, another 2–3 minutes, or until the chicken livers are just cooked through and most of the liquid in the skillet has evaporated. Remove from the heat and allow the chicken livers to cool to room temperature.

Place the skillet ingredients in a food processor. Add the remaining butter and process until smooth. Season with salt and pepper. Spoon the pâté into a bowl, tightly cover, and place in the fridge for several hours or overnight to allow the flavours to meld.

Allow the pâté to stand at room temperature for 30 minutes before spreading or piping it on the toasted baguette rounds. Garnish each with a few sliced gherkins and a parsley sprig.

FOR TOASTED BAGUETTE ROUNDS

Cut the baguette into $1/4$-inch-thick (5-mm) slices. Place them in a single layer on a baking tray and bake in a 400°F (200°C) oven for 10–12 minutes, or until lightly toasted.

ERIC'S OPTIONS
If you can find them, replace the chicken livers in this recipe with an equal amount of duck livers. Melba toast or good-quality crackers could replace the toasted baguette rounds. For a sweet and spicy taste, top the pâté with red pepper jelly or chutney instead of gherkins.

ROASTED PEPPER ANTIPASTO
on PARMESAN TOASTS

preparation time · 15 minutes
cooking time · 10 minutes
makes · 16–20 pieces

To quickly whip up this recipe, use the roasted red peppers sold in tins or jars in most supermarkets. Or, if you have time, roast your own (see next page).

ERIC'S OPTIONS
To make this appetizing bite a little richer, spread the toast with a little goat cheese before topping with antipasto.

16–20	baguette rounds sliced 1/4 inch (5 mm) thick	16–20
	olive oil for baguette slices	
1/4 cup	freshly grated Parmesan cheese	50 mL
2	large roasted red peppers, cut into thin strips	2
1/3 cup	coarsely chopped sun-dried tomatoes	75 mL
2 Tbsp.	capers	25 mL
2	garlic cloves, finely chopped	2
1/4 cup	olive oil	50 mL
2 Tbsp.	chopped fresh basil or oregano	25 mL
to taste	salt and freshly cracked black pepper	to taste
16–20	small basil leaves or oregano sprigs	16–20

Preheat the oven to 400°F (200°C). Brush the bread slices lightly with olive oil and then sprinkle with the cheese. Bake until lightly toasted, about 10 minutes.

Combine the red peppers, tomatoes, capers, garlic, olive oil, chopped basil or oregano, salt and pepper in a bowl. When it is time to serve, mound the mixture on the baguette rounds. Garnish with the basil leaves or oregano sprigs and serve immediately.

ROASTING PEPPERS

Store-bought roasted peppers are convenient, but if you have the time, roast your own. They will be far more flavourful as they aren't packed in the taste-diluting water of the tinned or jarred variety. When choosing fresh bell peppers, look for evenly shaped peppers that feel heavy for their size; these are indicators of thick, sweet flesh that is easier to peel. Buy red, orange or yellow peppers; the green ones, because of their tougher skin and thin flesh, are not well-suited for roasting and peeling.

Preheat the oven to 450°F (230°F). Lightly brush the peppers with olive oil and place in a shallow-sided baking dish or roasting pan. Roast them, turning them from time to time, until they begin to char and blister. This should take about 20–25 minutes. Remove from the oven, cover with foil and cool to room temperature. When they are cool, peel off the skin; it should slip away easily. Cut the peppers in half and carefully remove the core and seeds. The peppers are now ready to use as desired. They will keep in the fridge in a tightly sealed jar for up to a week.

PORK and CRAB
POT STICKERS

preparation time · 30–40 minutes
cooking time · 4–5 minutes per batch
makes · 36–40 pot stickers

These small, Asian-style dumplings are so named because when they're done, the reduced, almost caramelized cooking liquid causes them to stick slightly to the pan.

THE SAUCE			
1 cup	rice vinegar	250 mL
2 Tbsp.	sugar	25 mL
1 Tbsp.	sesame oil	15 mL
2	thinly sliced green onions	2
1/4 cup	soy sauce	50 mL
1	small carrot, grated	1

THE POT STICKERS			
1/2 lb.	ground pork	250 g
1 cup	fresh or tinned crabmeat (drained well)	250 mL
2	green onions, finely chopped	2
2	garlic cloves, crushed	2
2 tsp.	grated fresh ginger	10 mL
2 Tbsp.	soy sauce	25 mL
1/2 cup	sliced water chestnuts, finely chopped	125 mL
1/4 cup	chopped cilantro (optional)	50 mL
1	large egg white	1
to taste	salt, pepper and Asian-style hot sauce	to taste
36–40	Chinese-style dumpling wrappers	36–40
	vegetable oil	

THE SAUCE
Combine all ingredients in a bowl and set aside until needed.

THE POT STICKERS
Combine the pork, crabmeat, green onions, garlic, ginger, soy sauce, water chestnuts, cilantro, if desired, and egg white in a bowl. Season with salt, pepper and hot sauce. Lay out 6 dumpling wrappers on your work surface. Brush the edges of the wrappers with cold water. Place 2 tsp. (10 mL) of filling in the centre of each wrapper. Fold each wrapper in half and press the edges together to seal in the filling. If desired, crimp the edges to give them a decorative look. Set the pot stickers on a non-stick or parchment-lined tray, ensuring that they do not touch. (If they do, they'll stick together.) Repeat with the remaining dumpling wrappers and filling. (Pot stickers can be frozen on the tray at this stage. When frozen solid, transfer them to freezer bags. When needed, remove from the bag and partially thaw them on trays, making sure they do not touch. Do not let them completely thaw or they will become soft and impossible to handle. Cook as described below.)

Heat 1 Tbsp. (15 mL) of oil in a large, heavy, non-stick skillet over medium-high heat. When the oil is hot, add the pot stickers, cooking 12–18 at a time, depending on the pan size. (Pot stickers can be kept warm in a 200°F/95°C oven until all are cooked. Or you can eat the first batch while waiting for the others to cook.) Cook until the pot stickers are golden brown on the bottom. Do not turn. Pour in 3–4 Tbsp. (45–60 mL) of water, being careful of splatters from the pan. Cover and cook 4–5 minutes more, gently swirling the pan from time to time. Remove the lid and continue cooking until the liquid has almost completely evaporated. Place the pot stickers, browned side up, on a tray. Serve with dipping sauce alongside.

NOTE
Chinese-style dumpling wrappers can be found in Asian food markets and in many mainstream supermarkets. Unused wrappers freeze well.

ERIC'S OPTIONS
Use ground chicken instead of pork, or replace the crab with coarsely chopped salad shrimp.

CARAMELIZED ONION and STILTON TARTS

preparation time ·	20 minutes	
cooking time ·	25–30 minutes	
makes ·	24 tarts	

You can use homemade or store-bought tart shells in this recipe. If you use the frozen store-bought shells, thaw them before filling and baking.

ERIC'S OPTIONS
The white part of a medium leek, washed, dried and finely chopped, could replace the onion. Leeks are related to garlic and onion, and add the flavour of both in a mild but not over-powering way. If you cannot find or afford Stilton, any blue cheese can replace it. If you do not care for blue-veined cheeses, use 1 cup (250 mL) of grated aged Cheddar cheese instead.

1 Tbsp.	butter	15 mL
1	medium onion, finely diced	1
24	2-inch (5-cm) unsweetened tart shells	24
2	large eggs, beaten	2
1 cup	light cream	250 mL
to taste	salt and white pepper	to taste
1/4 lb	Stilton cheese, crumbled	125 g

Melt the butter in a small skillet over medium-low heat. Add the onion and cook until it is sticky and a rich golden colour, about 10 minutes. Remove from the heat and cool.

In a small bowl combine the eggs, cream, salt and pepper. Place the tart shells on a large baking tray. Place a small amount of onion in each shell. Pour in enough egg mixture to almost reach the top of the shell. Top each with a little crumbled Stilton. Bake in a preheated 375°F (190°C) oven for 25–30 minutes, or until lightly puffed and golden brown. (The tarts can be made a day in advance, cooled and stored in the fridge. Reheat in a 375°F (190°C) oven for 10–15 minutes.)

Fettuccini with Chicken, Pesto and Cherry Tomatoes, 49

Tortilla Chips
with Shrimp and
Corn Salsa, 3

Greek-Style
Mini Burgers
on Cucumber
Rounds, 5

Asparagus, Roasted Pepper
and Mushroom Strudel, 80

Romaine with
Oranges, Feta
and Olives, 19

Organic Greens with Pears,
Pecans and Crumbled Stilton, 18

Tomato and
Goat Cheese
Salad, 25

Chilled Beet
Soup, 43

Pork and Crab
Pot Stickers, 14

Curried
Vegetable
Stew, 90

Portobello Mushroom Burgers
with Lemon Basil Mayonnaise, 84

Prawn
Bisque, 40

SUMPTUOUS SALADS

CHAPTER TWO

Organic Greens with Pears, Pecans and Crumbled Stilton 18

Romaine with Oranges, Feta and Olives 19

Light and Delicious Caesar Salad 20

Spring Vegetable Salad 22

Roasted Pepper and Spinach Salad 24

Tomato and Goat Cheese Salad 25

Plum Tomato, Onion and Caper Salad 26

Southern-Spiced Coleslaw with Jicama and Corn 27

Yam Salad with Red Onions, Black Beans and Cilantro 28

Moroccan-Spiced Potato and Carrot Salad 29

Tropical Shrimp Salad 30

ORGANIC GREENS with PEARS, PECANS and CRUMBLED STILTON

preparation time	·	15 minutes
cooking time	·	none
makes	·	4 servings

To return the organic baby salad greens to a crisp, fresh-picked state, soak them in ice-cold water for 30 minutes, then drain and dry them before adding them to the salad.

ERIC'S OPTIONS
Replace the pear with sliced apple, or use regular blue cheese instead of Stilton.

2 Tbsp.	balsamic vinegar	25 mL
3 Tbsp.	extra virgin olive oil	45 mL
to taste	salt and freshly cracked black pepper	to taste
6 cups	organic baby salad greens	1.5 L
2	ripe pears, cored and sliced	2
1/2 cup	pecan halves	125 mL
1/3 cup	crumbled Stilton cheese	75 mL

Whisk together the vinegar, oil, salt and pepper in a salad bowl. Add the salad greens and gently toss to combine. Arrange on 4 plates. Arrange the sliced pears, pecans and cheese on the greens. Drizzle any dressing left in the salad bowl over top. Serve immediately.

ROMAINE with ORANGES, FETA and OLIVES

preparation time	·	10 minutes
cooking time	·	none
makes	·	4 servings

This Mediterranean-style salad bursts with colour and flavour. Serve it as a starter or a side dish for grilled fish, pork or poultry. It is particularly nice with Heavenly Spiced Turkey and Vegetable Kebabs (page 108).

ERIC'S OPTIONS
Replace the romaine with an equal amount of spinach leaves or baby salad greens. A sprinkling of capers is also nice in this salad. Replace regular oranges with blood oranges when available.

3 Tbsp.	orange juice	45 mL
2 Tbsp.	red wine vinegar	25 mL
3 Tbsp.	olive oil	45 mL
1/2 tsp.	sugar	2 mL
to taste	salt and freshly cracked black pepper	to taste
3	medium oranges, peeled, halved and sliced	3
3/4 cup	crumbled feta cheese	175 mL
20–24	whole black or green olives	20–24
2	ripe medium tomatoes, cut into small wedges	2
6 cups	chopped romaine lettuce	1.5 L
1	small red onion, thinly sliced	1

Whisk together the orange juice, vinegar, oil, sugar, salt and pepper in a salad bowl. Add the remaining salad ingredients and gently toss. Divide among plates or serve on a large platter, ensuring some of the oranges, cheese, olives, onions and tomatoes decorate the top.

LIGHT and DELICIOUS CAESAR SALAD

preparation time	·	15 minutes
cooking time	·	10–15 minutes
makes	·	4 servings

Here's a lower-fat — no mayonnaise, no egg, no oil — version of the classic salad. The yogurt in the dressing adds a refreshing tanginess.

ERIC'S OPTIONS
If you love olive or focaccia bread, use either of them to make the croutons instead of baguette. If you do not care for anchovies, simply omit them.

1/4	baguette, cut into small cubes	1/4
3	garlic cloves, crushed	3
2 tsp.	Dijon mustard	10 mL
1/2 tsp.	sugar	2 mL
1/3 cup	2% yogurt	75 mL
1 tsp.	anchovy paste	5 mL
2 tsp.	red wine vinegar	10 mL
2 Tbsp.	lemon juice	25 mL
2 tsp.	Worcestershire sauce	10 mL
1/2 tsp.	hot pepper sauce	2 mL
to taste	salt and freshly cracked black pepper	to taste
1	medium head romaine lettuce, chopped, washed and dried	1
1/4 cup	freshly grated Parmesan cheese	50 mL
4	lemon slices or wedges	4

Preheat the oven to 400°F (200°C). Place the baguette cubes on a non-stick or parchment-lined baking tray. Bake for 10–15 minutes, or until tightly toasted.

Place the garlic, mustard, sugar, yogurt, anchovy paste, vinegar, lemon juice, Worcestershire sauce, hot pepper sauce, salt and pepper in a large bowl and whisk well to combine. Toss in the lettuce, croutons and half the cheese. Divide the salad among 4 plates. Sprinkle with the remaining cheese, garnish with the lemon, and serve immediately.

PREPARING LETTUCE FOR THE SALAD BOWL

Improperly washing and drying lettuce will give your salad a limp texture and a water-drowned taste. Place trimmed, whole lettuce leaves into a large bowl of cold water. Gently swirl to remove any dirt. Allow the leaves to rise to the surface; the dirt will sink to the bottom. If your lettuce was a little limp, leave it in the water for a few minutes to crisp up. Dry the lettuce in a salad spinner or on towels, tearing into pieces or chopping if necessary. Do not use a salad spinner to dry the more delicate leaves, such as butter lettuce, as they can easily bruise.

SPRING VEGETABLE SALAD

preparation time ·	10 minutes	
cooking time ·	none	
makes ·	4–6 servings	

Nowadays the vegetables used in this salad are available year-round. But they are at their best when harvested in season from a farm or backyard garden near you. This salad would make a nice accompaniment for Asparagus, Roasted Pepper and Mushroom Strudel (page 80).

ERIC'S OPTIONS
Make the dressing and prepare the vegetables early in the day, refrigerate, and toss them together just before serving.

2 tsp.	Dijon mustard	10 mL
1 Tbsp.	chopped fresh parsley	15 mL
1 1/2 Tbsp.	red wine vinegar	20 mL
1/4 cup	extra virgin olive oil	50 mL
1/2 tsp.	sugar	2 mL
to taste	salt and freshly cracked black pepper	to taste
1	bunch spinach, stemmed, washed and dried	1
1	bunch radishes, trimmed, washed and thinly sliced	1
4	green onions cut into 1-inch (2.5-cm) pieces	4
1	medium carrot, thinly sliced	1
1/2	English cucumber, halved lengthwise and sliced	1/2

Whisk together the mustard, parsley, vinegar, oil, sugar, salt and pepper in a salad bowl. Add the vegetables and toss to coat with the dressing. Arrange the salad on plates, ensuring some of the sliced vegetables appear on top. Serve immediately.

SALAD DRESSING 101

When making a salad dressing, be generous with flavourings, such as salt, pepper, herbs and spices. A highly flavoured dressing can be added more sparingly, thus reducing the amount of oil in the salad. Salads are primarily composed of vegetables with a high water content, such as lettuce, are prone to wilting and should be dressed just before serving. Those that are designed to absorb the dressing ingredients, such as potato- or pasta-based salads, will benefit if they are dressed a few hours before serving to allow the flavours to develop. Always consider food safety when preparing, storing and serving salads. Keep salads and dressings with ingredients that could develop bacteria quickly, such as meat, poultry, eggs, fish and dairy products, well chilled. Make sure they are kept refrigerated until serving time, and refrigerate leftovers promptly.

ROASTED PEPPER and SPINACH SALAD

preparation time · 15 minutes
cooking time · 10–15 minutes
makes · 4 servings

This salad goes well with simply prepared fish, poultry or meat. Try it with Honey and Citrus-Glazed Chicken Breast (page 97) or Prosciutto-Wrapped Pork Loin with Salsa Verde (page 133). You can use store-bought or homemade roasted peppers in this recipe (see page 13 for homemade).

ERIC'S OPTIONS
Use 1/3 cup (75 mL) of whole, toasted almonds instead of the pine nuts. Substitute 4–6 cups (1–1.5 L) of chopped romaine for the spinach.

1/4 cup	extra virgin olive oil	50 mL
2 Tbsp.	balsamic vinegar	25 mL
1 tsp.	Dijon mustard	5 mL
to taste	salt and freshly cracked black pepper	to taste
1	bunch fresh spinach, trimmed, washed, and dried	1
1	large roasted red pepper, seeded and thinly sliced	1
1/2 cup	thinly shaved Parmesan cheese	125 mL
3 Tbsp.	toasted pine nuts	45 mL

Place the oil, vinegar, mustard, salt and pepper in a salad bowl and whisk well to combine. Add the spinach and toss to coat with the dressing. Divide among 4 plates. Top with the remaining ingredients and serve.

TOASTING NUTS
Toasting nuts and seeds, such as pine nuts and unroasted almonds, cashews or peanuts, gives them a richer, more robust taste. Place in a single layer on a baking sheet. Bake in a preheated 350°F (180°C) oven for 10–15 minutes, or until lightly toasted. Shake the pan from time to time and watch them carefully so they don't burn. Cool to room temperature before using. Toasted nuts are great sprinkled on salads, pastas, Asian-style noodle dishes, and desserts such as cakes and ice cream.

TOMATO and GOAT
CHEESE SALAD

preparation time ·	15 minutes
cooking time ·	none
makes ·	4–6 servings

A mix between a salad and an appetizer, this dish is best served on a platter and shared in a casual way with your dinner companions. All you need is a loaf of crusty bread to mound the tomatoes and cheese on.

ERIC'S OPTIONS
Replace the tomatoes with a selection of sliced, grilled vegetables, such as zucchini, onions, peppers, mushrooms and eggplant. Lightly brush vegetables with olive oil and season with salt and freshly cracked black pepper to taste. Grill over medium-high heat until just tender. Cooking times will vary from vegetable to vegetable.

5 oz.	round or log of fresh goat cheese	150 g
4–6	vine-ripened tomatoes (choose a selection of colours if available)	4–6
12–16	fresh basil leaves, torn into smaller pieces if large	12–16
1/2 cup	black olives	125 mL
1/4 cup	extra virgin olive oil	50 mL
to taste	salt and freshly cracked black pepper	to taste

Place the cheese in the centre of a serving platter. Cut the tomatoes into thin slices and place them in an over-lapping pattern around the cheese. Disperse the basil and olives over top. Liberally pour the olive oil (1/4 cup/50 mL should do), over the tomatoes and cheese. Sprinkle with salt and pepper. Let stand 10 minutes to allow the juices from the tomatoes to combine with the olive oil.

PLUM TOMATO, ONION and CAPER SALAD

preparation time · 10 minutes
cooking time · none
makes · 6–8 side dish servings

This quick-to-prepare salad goes well with seafood, such as Baked Chilled Salmon Fillets with Dill and Horseradish Sauce (page 62).

ERIC'S OPTIONS
Use a mix of different-coloured, similar-sized ripe tomatoes instead of the plum tomatoes.

1 tsp.	dried tarragon	5 mL
1/3 cup	extra virgin olive oil	75 mL
1 Tbsp.	Dijon mustard	15 mL
to taste	salt and freshly cracked black pepper	to taste
1/4 cup	capers, plus 1 Tbsp (15 mL) of their juice	50 mL
8	ripe plum tomatoes, cut into wedges	8
1	medium white onion, thinly sliced	1

Whisk together the tarragon, oil, mustard, salt and pepper in a bowl. Add the capers, tomatoes and onions and mix gently. Allow the salad to marinate for 30 minutes at room temperature before serving.

SOUTHERN-SPICED COLESLAW
with JICAMA and CORN

preparation time	·	15 minutes
cooking time	·	none
makes	·	6–8 side dish servings

Jicama, sold at most supermarkets, is a bulbous root with a crunchy white flesh that can be eaten raw or cooked. This salad goes well with Cornmeal-Crusted Chicken Legs (page 98).

NOTE
Store leftover jicama in a plastic bag in the fridge. Peeled and then sliced or cubed, jicama can be added to a green salad or vegetable and dip tray, or tossed into a vegetable stir-fry.

ERIC'S OPTIONS
For added richness, add 1/3 cup (75 mL) of coarsely chopped pecans to the coleslaw. For a less spicy taste, remove and discard the jalapeño seeds before chopping; they contain much of the pepper's heat.

1	fresh or canned jalapeño pepper, finely chopped	1
1/3 cup	vegetable oil	75 mL
2	limes, juiced	2
2 tsp.	ground cumin	10 mL
2 tsp.	chili powder	10 mL
2 tsp.	sugar	10 mL
to taste	salt and freshly cracked black pepper	to taste
1/2	small head red cabbage, cored and shredded	1/2
1/2	medium jicama, peeled and cut into thin strips	1/2
1 cup	fresh cooked or frozen (thawed) corn kernels	250 mL

Place the jalapeño, oil, lime juice, cumin, chili powder, sugar, salt and pepper in a bowl and whisk well. Mix in the remaining ingredients. Cover and refrigerate for an hour before serving to allow the flavours to meld.

YAM SALAD with RED ONIONS, BLACK BEANS and CILANTRO

preparation time	·	20 minutes
cooking time	·	10–15 minutes
makes	·	4–6 side dish servings

Here's a funky, sweet and spicy spin on the classic potato salad. Serve it with Southern-Style Short Ribs (page 114) or Pork Side Ribs with Chipotle Barbecue Sauce (page 134).

NOTE
See "Sweet Potatoes and Yams" (page 149). Black beans are sold alongside other tinned legumes, such as kidney beans, in most supermarkets.

ERIC'S OPTIONS
If you're not a fan of cilantro, replace it with an equal amount of chopped green onion.

2 lbs.	yams (about 2 medium), peeled and cut into 1-inch (2.5-cm) cubes	1 kg
1/2	medium red onion, halved and thinly sliced	1/2
1 cup	rinsed and well-drained canned black beans	250 mL
1/4 cup	chopped cilantro	50 mL
3 Tbsp.	olive oil	45 mL
1	lime, juiced	1
pinch	cayenne pepper, ground allspice and ground nutmeg	pinch
to taste	salt and freshly cracked black pepper	to taste

Place the yams in a pot and cover with cold water. Bring to a gentle boil and cook until they are just tender. Remove from the heat and drain well. Place in a large bowl with the remaining ingredients. Gently mix until combined. Serve warm or at room temperature.

MOROCCAN-SPICED POTATO and CARROT SALAD

preparation time · 15 minutes
cooking time · 15 minutes
makes · 6 side dish servings

This mildly spiced, invitingly fragrant salad compliments Mediterranean and Middle Eastern–style meats, chicken and fish. Try it with Lemony Lamb Chops with Artichokes, Olives and Mint (page 132).

ERIC'S OPTIONS
A nice addition to this salad is 1/2 cup (125 mL) of whole black or green olives. You can substitute 1 tsp. (5 mL) of dried mint for the fresh.

1 lb.	carrots, cut into 1/2-inch (1-cm) coins	500 g
1 lb.	white or red-skinned potatoes, cut into 1/2-inch (1-cm) cubes	500 g
1	lemon, juiced	1
1/4 cup	olive oil	50 mL
1 tsp.	sugar	5 mL
2 tsp.	ground cumin	10 mL
2 tsp.	paprika	10 mL
1/4 tsp.	cayenne pepper	1 mL
2	garlic cloves, crushed	2
to taste	salt and freshly cracked black pepper	to taste
3	green onions, finely chopped	3
3 Tbsp.	chopped fresh mint	45 mL

Boil the carrots and potatoes until firm tender. Combine the remaining ingredients in a large bowl, mixing well. Drain the carrots and potatoes and, while still hot, toss them with the dressing. Adjust the seasoning with salt and pepper. Serve hot or at room temperature.

TROPICAL SHRIMP SALAD

preparation time · 30 minutes
cooking time · none
makes · 4 servings

This vibrant salad makes a light and inviting summer meal. Or serve it in winter when the snow is falling and you're looking for a taste of the tropics.

NOTE
See "Buying and Storing Fresh Fish and Shellfish" (page 61).

ERIC'S OPTIONS
Replace the papaya with a large ripe mango or 2 smaller ones. If you don't have fresh tarragon, substitute 1/2 tsp. (2 mL) of dried. Cooked scallops, crab or lobster meat can replace the shrimp—or try a combination of cooked seafood.

1	ripe papaya, halved, seeded, peeled and cut into 16 wedges	1
2	ripe avocados, halved, pitted, peeled and each cut into 12 wedges	2
1	large grapefruit, peel and pith removed, halved and thinly sliced crosswise	1
2	Belgian endives, cored and separated into leaves	2
3/4 lb.	small cooked shrimp (see page 77)	375 g
1/2 cup	yogurt	125 mL
1/2 cup	light sour cream	125 mL
2 Tbsp.	tarragon or white wine vinegar	25 mL
1 tsp.	honey, or to taste	5 mL
1 Tbsp.	chopped fresh tarragon	15 mL
to taste	salt and white pepper	to taste

Arrange the papaya, avocados, grapefruit and endive in a spoke-like fashion on 4 dinner plates. Divide the shrimp into 4 servings and mound in the centre of each plate. Combine the remaining ingredients in a bowl, mixing well. Drizzle the dressing on the salads, or serve it alongside.

Carrot, Garlic and Chive Soup — 32

Summer Harvest Soup — 34

Creamy Corn Soup — 36

Cauliflower Soup with Curry and Coconut Milk — 37

Five-Onion Soup — 38

Tortellini Soup with Italian Sausage and Crumbled Feta — 39

SEASONAL SOUPS

CHAPTER THREE

Prawn Bisque — 40

Cabbage Soup with Smoked Turkey and Rosemary — 42

Chilled Beet Soup — 43

Cold Strawberry Soup with Mint and Black Pepper — 44

CARROT, GARLIC and CHIVE SOUP

preparation time	·	30 minutes
cooking time	·	25 minutes
makes	·	6 servings

This simple soup made it onto the *Ottawa Citizen's* "reader's choice" best recipe list in 2000. Although it's an everyday kind of soup, it can also provide a festive way to start a special meal.

ERIC'S OPTIONS
If you're vegetarian, replace the chicken stock with a vegetable-based one. Substitute soy milk for the whipping cream if you do not eat dairy products. For added spice, add 2 tsp. (10 mL) of freshly grated ginger and 1 Tbsp. (15 mL) of curry powder when sautéing the carrots.

2 Tbsp.	vegetable oil	25 mL
1	medium onion, sliced	1
6	garlic cloves, chopped	6
3 cups	sliced carrots	750 mL
2 Tbsp.	all-purpose flour	25 mL
5 cups	chicken stock	1.25 L
1/2 cup	whipping cream	125 mL
2–3 Tbsp.	chopped fresh chives	25–45 mL
to taste	salt and freshly cracked black pepper	to taste

Heat the oil in a pot over medium heat. Add the onion, garlic and carrots and cook until the vegetables are slightly softened, about 5 minutes. Mix in the flour until well combined. While stirring, slowly pour in the stock and bring to a simmer. Cook until the carrots are very tender, about 20 minutes.

Working in batches, purée the mixture in a blender or food processor. (The soup can be prepared to this stage a day or two in advance. Cool to room temperature and store in the refrigerator until needed.) Return the soup to the pot and bring it back to a simmer. Stir in the cream and chives, reserving a few for garnish. Season with salt and pepper. When the soup is heated through pour it into bowls and sprinkle with the reserved chives before serving.

MAKING STOCK

You can buy good quality, ready to use stock, but if you have the time, making your own can give you a richer stock tailored to your own taste, and you will know exactly what goes into it.

For vegetable stock, slice two medium peeled carrots, two medium peeled onions, two celery ribs, two medium tomatoes and 1/3 lb. (170 g) white or brown mushrooms and place in a tall stockpot. Add a bay leaf, a few whole black peppercorns and a few sprigs of fresh parsley and thyme (or 1 tsp./5 mL dried). Add 10–12 cups (2.5–3 L) of cold water. Bring to a gentle simmer and cook uncovered for 1 1/2–2 hours, or until the mixture has a pleasing vegetable flavour. Strain, cool and refrigerate.

For fish, chicken or beef stock, place 2–3 pounds (1–1.5 kg) of bones in a tall stockpot. Use the same vegetables and herbs as for vegetable stock, but reduce the carrot and onion to 1 each. The tomatoes and mushrooms are optional. To add colour to chicken or beef stock, roast the bones and vegetables in a hot oven until golden brown, about 30 minutes, before placing in the stockpot. For fish stock, it is best to use white fish bones as bones from fish such as salmon can give the stock a strong, oily taste. Fish stock cooks quickly, so slice the vegetables thinly to better release the flavour into the stock.

Add enough cold water to completely cover the bones and vegetables, about 10–12 cups (2.5–3 L) depending on the size and width of the pot. Simmer fish stock for 30–45 minutes; chicken stock for 1 1/2–2 hours; and beef stock 3–4 hours. Skim off any foam that rises to the top as it cooks and add additional water as needed. Before straining, taste the stock to see if it has reached its flavour potential. Remember that the stock isn't seasoned like the store-bought variety; add salt and pepper to a small amount of stock before sampling. Cool to room temperature, cover and refrigerate until needed.

Stock can be stored in the refrigerator for 2–3 days. Remove any fat from the surface of the stock before using. Stock also freezes well; divide it into portions you are likely to use in cooking before freezing.

SUMMER HARVEST SOUP

preparation time ·	30 minutes	
cooking time ·	25 minutes	
makes ·	6 servings	

Make this soup when your garden or your local market is offering a bounty of fresh, seasonal produce.

NOTE
Diced vegetables are usually cut into cubes of approximately ¼ inch (5 mm). For this soup you can make the cubes ½ inch (1 cm).

ERIC'S OPTIONS
Take advantage of fresh vegetables in the summer and double or triple this recipe. Freeze it and reheat it on an autumn day for a delicious reminder of summer. Substitute any summer vegetables, such as green beans, wax beans or summer squash, for those that do not appeal to you.

2–3 Tbsp.	olive oil	25–45 mL
1	medium onion, diced	1
1	medium carrot, diced	1
1	medium zucchini, diced	1
1	green or red bell pepper, diced	1
2	garlic cloves, chopped	2
4	ripe tomatoes, halved, seeds removed and diced	4
5 cups	chicken or vegetable stock	1.25 L
¼ cup	mixed chopped fresh herbs, such as dill, parsley, basil or oregano	50 mL
to taste	salt and freshly cracked black pepper	to taste

Heat the oil in a pot over medium heat and add the onion, carrot, zucchini, bell pepper and garlic. Cook, stirring, for 4–5 minutes. Add the tomatoes and stock and simmer for 20 minutes, or until the vegetables are tender. Mix in the herbs and season with salt and pepper. Thin with a little more stock if you find the soup is too thick.

FREEZING SOUP

To make more efficient use of freezer space, freeze soup in resealable plastic bags, rather than in bulky plastic containers. Freeze it in portions that suit your needs. To fill the bags more easily, set a bag in a container large enough to hold it once it's filled. Fold the top of the bag over the rim of the container to hold it in place. Pour in the soup, being careful not to overfill the bag, and then seal. Place the filled bags flat on a tray and freeze them solid. Label and date them and stack them in the freezer. Freeze for up to two months. Thaw the soup in the fridge overnight, placing the bag in a bowl just in case it leaks.

CREAMY CORN SOUP

preparation time · 20 minutes
cooking time · 30 minutes
makes · 6 servings

This soup is at its finest when fresh, local corn is in season.

ERIC'S OPTIONS
When fresh corn is not available, substitute 1½ cups (375 mL) of frozen corn kernels. Thaw before using and drain off any excess liquid. Do not cook the corn with the onions, as it is already partially cooked—add the corn along with the stock.

2 Tbsp.	olive oil	25 mL
3	cobs corn, kernels removed	3
1	small onion, diced	1
2	garlic cloves, chopped	2
5 cups	chicken or vegetable stock	1.25 L
½ tsp	dried thyme	2 mL
2	medium potatoes, peeled and cubed	2
1	bay leaf	1
½ cup	whipping cream or milk	125 mL
to taste	salt and freshly cracked black pepper	to taste
	chopped green onions or chives	

Heat the oil in a pot over medium heat and add the corn kernels, onion and garlic. Cook until just tender, about 5 minutes. Add the stock, thyme, potatoes and bay leaf. Simmer the soup until the potatoes are quite tender, about 20 minutes. Remove the bay leaf and purée the soup in a blender or food processor. Return it to the pot, add the cream or milk and bring the soup to a simmer (do not boil). Season with salt and pepper. Pour the soup into heated bowls, sprinkle with the green onions or chives and serve.

CAULIFLOWER SOUP with CURRY and COCONUT MILK

preparation time · 10 minutes
cooking time · 25–30 minutes
makes · 4 servings

Spicy curry and the silky richness of coconut milk turn ordinary tasting cauliflower into a soup that's a treat down to the last spoonful.

ERIC'S OPTIONS
Adjust the amount of curry powder to your taste: use less if you like a mild curry, more if you like things spicy. If you do not care for cilantro, replace it with finely chopped green onions. Try this soup with small broccoli florets instead of cauliflower.

3 Tbsp.	vegetable oil	45 mL
1	medium onion, finely chopped	1
2	garlic cloves, chopped	2
2 Tbsp.	curry powder	25 mL
3 Tbsp.	all-purpose flour	45 mL
3 cups	chicken stock	750 mL
1	14-oz. (398-mL) can light coconut milk	1
2 1/2 cups	small cauliflower florets	625 mL
1/4 cup	chopped cilantro	50 mL
to taste	salt and freshly cracked black pepper	to taste

Heat the oil in a pot over medium heat. Add the onion and garlic and cook for 2–3 minutes. Add the curry powder and cook, stirring for 2–3 minutes more. Stir in the flour. Slowly whisk in the chicken stock. Stir in the coconut milk, bring to a simmer and cook for 10 minutes. Add the cauliflower and cook for 10 minutes more, or until tender. Stir in the cilantro, season with salt and pepper and serve.

FIVE-ONION
SOUP

preparation time · 20 minutes
cooking time · 40 minutes
makes · 4 servings

If you love onions, you'll love this soup.

ERIC'S OPTIONS
To serve this soup in the style of French onion soup, serve in heat proof bowls and top each with a toasted round of French bread. Sprinkle with grated Swiss cheese and broil until the cheese is melted and golden brown.

3 Tbsp.	butter or olive oil	45 mL
2	medium onions, halved and thinly sliced	2
3	shallots, halved and thinly sliced	3
1	medium leek, white part only, halved lengthwise, washed well, and thinly sliced	1
2	garlic cloves, chopped	2
1 tsp.	dried thyme	5 mL
5 cups	beef, chicken or vegetable stock	1.25 L
to taste	salt and freshly cracked black pepper	to taste
2-3	green onions, chopped	2–3

Heat the butter or oil in a pot over medium heat and add the onions, shallots, leek and garlic. Cook for 10 minutes, until all are soft and a rich golden colour. Add the thyme and stock and gently simmer for 30 minutes. Season with salt and pepper, stir in the green onions and serve.

TORTELLINI SOUP with ITALIAN SAUSAGE and CRUMBLED FETA

preparation time · 15 minutes
cooking time · 10 minutes
makes · 4–6 servings

Fresh tortellini comes in a range of flavours and colours, but cheese or meat-filled tortellini works best in this Italian-style soup. If you prefer a spicy soup, choose hot sausage rather than the mild ones.

NOTE
Roast or grill the sausages, rather than pan-frying, as it gives them a nice even colour and does not require extra oil.

ERIC'S OPTIONS
Use fresh, small ravioli or agnolotti (half moon–shaped pasta) instead of the tortellini. Fresh chorizo can be substituted for the Italian sausage.

6 cups	chicken stock	1.5 L
2–3	garlic cloves, thinly sliced	2–3
1	12-oz. (350-g) package fresh tortellini	1
4	Italian sausages, cooked, cooled and thinly sliced	4
1 cup	crumbled feta cheese	250 mL
1/4 cup	chopped fresh basil or parsley	50 mL
to taste	salt and freshly cracked black pepper	to taste

Place the stock and garlic in a pot and bring to a gentle simmer. Meanwhile, bring a large pot of lightly salted water to a boil. Add the tortellini and cook until tender, about 8–10 minutes. Drain well and divide among the soup bowls. Divide the sliced sausage, cheese and chopped herbs among the bowls. Season the stock with salt and pepper, pour over the other ingredients and serve.

PRAWN
BISQUE

preparation time · 30 minutes
cooking time · 50 minutes
makes · 4 servings

Here's a luscious seafood soup that's a little less costly than its sister soup, lobster bisque. Serve it on special occasions — such as Wednesday night!

ERIC'S OPTIONS
To elegantly garnish this soup, top each serving with a whole cooked prawn. This rich, creamy soup makes a fine sauce for other seafood, such as grilled or pan-seared halibut or scallops, or a seafood pasta dish.

16	medium tiger prawns (see page 77)	16
3 Tbsp.	olive oil	45 mL
1	garlic clove, thinly sliced	1
1	small carrot, thinly sliced	1
1	celery stalk, thinly sliced	1
1	small onion, thinly sliced	1
1 tsp.	dried tarragon	5 mL
1	bay leaf	1
1 Tbsp.	tomato paste	15 mL
1/2 cup	dry white wine	125 mL
3 1/2 cups	chicken, fish, or vegetable stock	875 mL
3 Tbsp.	all-purpose flour	45 mL
1/2 cup	whipping cream	125 mL
to taste	salt, white pepper and cayenne pepper	to taste
1/4 cup	warm brandy (optional)	50 mL
1 Tbsp.	chopped fresh parsley or chives	15 mL

Peel the prawns, reserving the shells. Coarsely chop the meat and set aside in the refrigerator.

Heat 2 Tbsp. (25 mL) of the oil in a pot over medium heat. Add the prawn shells, garlic, carrot, celery and onion. Cook, stirring occasionally, for 5–8 minutes, until the shells are bright red and almost crispy. Add the tarragon, bay leaf, tomato paste, wine and 3 cups (750 mL) of the stock. Gently simmer for 30–40 minutes.

Strain the mixture into another pot, then bring it back to a simmer. Mix the flour with the remaining 1/2 cup (125 mL) of stock until it is smooth. Slowly pour this mixture, whisking continually, into the simmering stock. Gently simmer until the flour has cooked through and the soup has lightly thickened, about 5 minutes. (The soup can be prepared to this stage a day in advance and kept refrigerated until needed.) Add the whipping cream and season with salt, pepper and cayenne. Keep the soup warm over medium-low heat.

Heat the remaining 1 Tbsp. (15 mL) oil in a small skillet over medium-high heat. Add the prawn pieces and cook until just cooked through, about 1–2 minutes. Divide the prawns and the brandy, if desired, among four heated soup bowls. Pour in the bisque, sprinkle with chopped parsley or chives, and serve.

CABBAGE SOUP with SMOKED TURKEY and ROSEMARY

preparation time · 20 minutes
cooking time · 35–45 minutes
makes · 6 servings

This hearty soup makes a good winter supper when accompanied by a loaf of fresh, home-style bread.

NOTE
Smoked turkey legs can be found at most supermarkets and butcher shops.

ERIC'S OPTIONS
Use 2 cups (500 mL) of cubed ham instead of the smoked turkey. If you do not have fresh rosemary, use 1 tsp. (5 mL) dried. Savoy cabbage can be substituted for green cabbage.

2 Tbsp.	butter	25 mL
1	medium onion, diced	1
2	garlic cloves, chopped	2
3 cups	chopped green cabbage	750 mL
1	medium carrot, halved and sliced	1
2 tsp.	chopped fresh rosemary	10 mL
1	small smoked turkey leg, meat removed and cubed	1
1	bay leaf	1
2	medium potatoes, peeled and cubed	2
6 cups	chicken stock	1.5 L
to taste	salt and freshly cracked black pepper	to taste
2–3 Tbsp.	chopped fresh parsley or green onions	25–45 mL

Melt the butter in a large pot over medium heat. Add the onion, garlic, cabbage and carrot and cook until softened, about 5 minutes. Add the rosemary, turkey, bay leaf, potatoes and stock. Gently simmer the soup for 30–40 minutes. Season with salt and pepper. Pour into bowls, sprinkle with parsley or green onions and serve.

CHILLED BEET SOUP

preparation time	·	20 minutes
cooking time	·	30 minutes
makes	·	4 servings

Balsamic vinegar, horseradish and honey give this refreshing soup a brilliant taste and colour. Serve it when you're looking for a cool, savoury start to a summer meal.

ERIC'S OPTIONS
For a dramatic presentation, bring the bowls of soup to the table in a large, attractive, deep-sided dish filled with ice. For a lower-fat alternative, use thick yogurt instead of sour cream.

1 lb.	beets, boiled until tender, cooled, peeled and sliced	500 g
2 1/2 cups	chicken or vegetable stock	625 mL
1 Tbsp.	horseradish	15 mL
2 Tbsp.	balsamic vinegar	25 mL
2 Tbsp.	honey	25 ml
to taste	salt and freshly cracked black pepper	to taste
	sour cream and dill sprigs	

Process the beets, stock, horseradish, vinegar, honey, salt and pepper in a blender or food processor until smooth. Refrigerate for at least 2 hours. Taste and adjust the seasoning if necessary. Ladle into well-chilled soup bowls. Garnish each serving with a dollop of sour cream and a dill sprig. Serve immediately.

COLD STRAWBERRY SOUP
with MINT and BLACK PEPPER

preparation time · 20 minutes
cooking time · none
makes · 4–6 servings

Spicy pepper, fragrant fresh mint and sweet strawberries combine to awaken the palate. A good starter for a meal served alfresco during strawberry season.

ERIC'S OPTIONS
Replace the mint with basil for a more savoury soup. For added richness, replace ½ the yogurt with light cream.

2 pints	strawberries, hulled	1 L
1 cup	yogurt	250 mL
1 cup	sour cream	250 mL
2 tsp.	honey	10 mL
1/4 cup	red wine vinegar	50 mL
to taste	salt	to taste
1 Tbsp.	chopped fresh mint	15 mL
1–2 tsp.	freshly cracked black pepper	5–10 mL

Reserve a few strawberries to garnish the top of the soup and place the remainder in a blender or food processor. Add the yogurt, sour cream, honey, vinegar and salt and process until smooth. Transfer to a bowl. Cover and refrigerate for at least 2 hours. Adjust the seasoning and gently mix before ladling the soup into well-chilled soup bowls. Slice the reserved strawberries and top the soup with the chopped fresh mint and a few strawberry slices. Sprinkle with freshly cracked black pepper. Serve immediately.

Rigatoni with Italian   46
Sausage, Peppers and Feta

Bow-Tie Pasta with Kale,   48
Anchovies and Parmesan

Fettuccini with Chicken,   49
Pesto and Cherry Tomatoes

Tomato, Prosciutto and Garlic-   50
Steamed Clams on Linguini

Spinach Tortellini with Creamy   51
Lemon and Leek Sauce

USING YOUR NOODLES

Roasted Vegetable Lasagna   52
with Ricotta Filling

Veal-Stuffed Pasta Shells   54
with Olive Tomato Sauce

Beef and Macaroni   56
Casserole

Grilled Sirloin on Rice Noodles with   58
Green Onions, Garlic and Ginger

CHAPTER FOUR

RIGATONI with ITALIAN SAUSAGE, PEPPERS and FETA

preparation time	·	20 minutes
cooking time	·	20 minutes
makes	·	4 servings

To efficiently prepare this dish, have all your ingredients cut and ready to go before you start cooking. Italian sausage is available in mild or hot versions; choose the type that suits your taste.

ERIC'S OPTIONS
If you prefer a tomato-based pasta sauce, substitute tomato sauce for chicken stock.

1 lb.	rigatoni or other bite-sized pasta	500 g
2 Tbsp.	olive oil	25 mL
1	medium onion, halved and sliced	1
1	small green bell pepper, seeded and thinly sliced	1
1	small red bell pepper, seeded and thinly sliced	1
2	garlic cloves, chopped	2
3	Italian sausages, cooked and sliced	3
1 cup	chicken stock	250 mL
2 Tbsp.	chopped fresh oregano, basil or parsley	25 mL
1/4 cup	freshly grated Parmesan cheese	50 mL
1 cup	crumbled feta cheese	250 mL
1/2 cup	black olives (optional)	125 mL
to taste	salt and freshly cracked black pepper	to taste

Cook the pasta in a large pot of boiling, salted water until just tender. While it is cooking, heat the oil in a large skillet over medium-high heat. Add the onion, bell peppers and garlic and cook until just tender, about 3–4 minutes. Add the sausages and stock and bring to a simmer. Reduce the heat to medium-low.

When the pasta is cooked, drain it, reserving 1/2 cup (125 mL) of the cooking liquid. Add the pasta, reserved cooking liquid and all the remaining ingredients to the skillet. Gently toss. Serve immediately.

COOKING PERFECT PASTA

To cook 1 pound (500 g) of fresh or dry pasta, the amount most often called for in recipes designed for four, bring 12 cups (3 litres) of water to a boil, then add 1 Tbsp. (15 mL) of salt. Salt in the cooking water heightens the flavour of pasta, particularly important if you are only tossing it with a few other ingredients, not bathing it in a rich sauce. The generous amount of water prevents the pasta from becoming overly starchy and sticking together as it cooks. (In the past, it was common practice to add a little oil to the pot to prevent this, but it is now thought oil coats the pasta and prevents the sauce from adhering to it.) Cook the pasta al dente — an Italian term which means to cook pasta or any other food until it offers a slight resistance when bitten into. Cooking time varies among the different types and brands of pasta. During cooking, taste the pasta to see how it is progressing.

BOW-TIE PASTA with KALE, ANCHOVIES and PARMESAN

preparation time · 20 minutes
cooking time · 15 minutes
makes · 4 servings

This pasta dish is a delicious way to incorporate vitamin- and mineral-rich kale into your diet.

NOTE
To blanch the kale, plunge it into boiling water and cook for 2 minutes. Remove and chill in cold water. Drain well.

ERIC'S OPTIONS
Other vitamin- and mineral-rich greens, such as spinach or chard, could replace the kale in this recipe.

1 lb.	bow-tie or other bite-sized pasta	500 g
2 Tbsp.	olive oil	25 mL
2	cloves garlic, chopped	2
1	medium onion, chopped	1
1	medium red bell pepper, seeded and cubed	1
2–3	anchovy fillets, finely chopped	2–3
pinch	crushed chili flakes	pinch
1	bunch kale, trimmed of tougher portions, blanched and chopped	1
1 cup	chicken or vegetable stock	250 mL
1/2 cup	freshly grated Parmesan cheese, plus more for the table	125 mL
to taste	salt and freshly cracked black pepper	to taste

Cook the pasta in a large pot of boiling, salted water until just tender. While the pasta is cooking, heat the olive oil in a large skillet over medium-high heat. Add the garlic, onion and red pepper and cook until just tender, about 3–4 minutes. Add the anchovies and chili flakes and cook 1 minute more. Add the kale and stock and bring to a simmer. Reduce the heat to medium-low.

Drain the pasta, reserving 1/2 cup (125 mL) of the cooking liquid. Add the pasta, reserved liquid and the Parmesan cheese to the skillet. Mix to combine. Season with salt and pepper. Spoon the pasta into individual serving bowls or onto a large platter. Serve with a bowl of extra Parmesan cheese on the side.

FETTUCCINI with CHICKEN, PESTO and CHERRY TOMATOES

preparation time	·	10 minutes
cooking time	·	10 minutes
makes	·	4 servings

Pesto imparts a delicious flavour to this simple, quickly made dish.

ERIC'S OPTIONS
For seafood lovers, the chicken in this recipe can be replaced with 20 medium-sized raw, peeled prawns (see page 77). Add them in place of the chicken, but only cook them for about 2 minutes, or until they are just cooked through.

1 lb.	fettuccini	500 g
2 Tbsp.	olive oil	25 mL
2–3	boneless, skinless, chicken breasts, thinly sliced	2–3
1 cup	pesto	250 mL
16	cherry tomatoes, halved	16
to taste	salt and freshly cracked black pepper	to taste
	freshly grated Parmesan cheese and extra virgin olive oil	
	small fresh basil leaves and toasted pine nuts for garnish (optional)	

Cook the pasta in a large pot of boiling, salted water until just tender. While it is cooking, heat the oil in a large skillet over medium-high heat. Add the chicken and season with salt and pepper. Cook, stirring, for 4–5 minutes, or until the chicken is just cooked. Stir in the pesto and cherry tomatoes and cook for 1–2 minutes more. Reduce the heat to medium-low.

Drain the pasta, reserving 1/2 cup (125 mL) of the cooking liquid. Add the pasta and reserved liquid to the skillet. Season with salt and pepper. Place the pasta in individual serving bowls or on a large platter. Sprinkle with the Parmesan cheese and drizzle a little extra virgin olive oil over top. If desired, garnish with basil leaves and toasted pine nuts.

TOMATO, PROSCIUTTO and GARLIC-STEAMED CLAMS on LINGUINI

preparation time · 10 minutes
cooking time · 10 minutes
makes · 4 servings

The prosciutto gives these clams an intriguing, Mediterranean-style taste. Because the prosciutto and clams are salty, freshly cracked black pepper is all you need to season this dish.

ERIC'S OPTIONS
Replace the clams with fresh mussels. Replace the linguini with fettuccini or spaghetti.

1 lb.	linguini	500 g
2 Tbsp.	olive oil	25 mL
1	medium onion, chopped	1
2	garlic cloves, chopped	2
4	slices prosciutto, finely chopped	4
1	28-oz. (796-mL) can diced tomatoes	1
1/2 cup	white wine	125 mL
to taste	freshly cracked black pepper	to taste
4 dozen	fresh clams (see page 61)	4 dozen
1/4 cup	chopped parsley or basil (or a mix of both)	50 mL
	freshly grated Parmesan cheese	

Cook the linguini in a large pot of boiling, salted water until just tender. While it is cooking, heat the oil in a large skillet over medium-high heat. Add the onion and garlic and cook until just tender, about 2–3 minutes. Add the prosciutto and cook 1 minute more. Add the tomatoes and wine and simmer for 5 minutes. Season with pepper. Add the clams, cover, and cook until they just open. Drain the linguini and divide among 4 bowls. Spoon the clams and sauce over the hot linguini. Sprinkle with chopped herbs and freshly grated Parmesan cheese.

SPINACH TORTELLINI with CREAMY LEMON and LEEK SAUCE

preparation time · 10 minutes
cooking time · 10–12 minutes
makes · 3–4 servings

The rich sauce gives this tortellini a gourmet touch. Consider this quick dish when you want to serve something special but are short on time. The recipe can be expanded if you're hosting a larger group.

ERIC'S OPTIONS
Use any other fresh filled pastas, such as ravioli or agnolotti, instead of tortellini.

1	12-oz. (350-g) package spinach tortellini, meat or cheese filled	1
2 Tbsp.	olive oil	25 mL
1	small leek, white part only, halved, washed, and thinly sliced	1
1	garlic clove, crushed	1
1/4 cup	lemon juice	50 mL
1 tsp.	finely grated lemon zest	5 mL
1 1/2 cups	whipping cream	375 mL
1/4 cup	freshly grated Parmesan cheese, plus more for the table	50 mL
to taste	salt and freshly cracked black pepper	to taste

Cook the tortellini in a large of pot of boiling, salted water until tender. While it is cooking, heat the oil in a large skillet over medium heat. Add the leek and garlic and cook until softened, about 4–5 minutes. Add the lemon juice and zest and cook until the lemon juice has almost evaporated. Add the cream and simmer until the sauce slightly thickens. Drain the cooked tortellini and add it to the skillet, along with the Parmesan cheese, salt and pepper. Mix to combine and simmer for 2 minutes more. Spoon into individual serving bowls or a deep platter.

ROASTED VEGETABLE LASAGNA
with RICOTTA FILLING

preparation time · 30–40 minutes
cooking time · 55–60 minutes
makes · 8 servings

Roasting the vegetables gives them a rich, almost sweet taste that nicely offsets the acidity of the tomatoes.

ERIC'S OPTIONS
Lasagna can be assembled in advance, wrapped in plastic wrap, stored in the refrigerator for up to a day, and baked later. Unbaked lasagna can also be frozen. Thaw it in the refrigerator overnight before baking as directed. To freeze cooked lasagna, cut it into portions, place in smaller baking dishes, wrap and freeze. Thaw in the fridge overnight before reheating in the oven or microwave. You may need to add a little water or tomato sauce to the dish to keep it moist if reheating in the oven.

2	medium onions, chopped	2
1	medium red or yellow bell pepper, cut into 1/2-inch (1-cm) cubes	1
1	small zucchini, quartered lengthwise and cut into 1/2-inch (1-cm) pieces	1
4–6	garlic cloves, thinly sliced	4–6
12	medium white or brown mushrooms, quartered	12
2 Tbsp.	olive oil	25 mL
1 tsp.	dried oregano	5 mL
to taste	salt and freshly cracked black pepper	to taste
1	28-oz. (796-mL) can diced tomatoes	1
1	28-oz. (796-mL) can crushed tomatoes	1
2 Tbsp.	tomato paste	25 mL
to taste	salt and freshly cracked black pepper	to taste
1/4 cup	pesto	50 mL
1	18-oz. (500-g) tub ricotta cheese	1
2	large eggs, beaten	2
1	18-oz. (500-g) box lasagna noodles, cooked as per package directions	1
3/4 lb.	mozzarella cheese, grated	375 g

Preheat the oven to 425°F (220°C). Place the onions, bell pepper, zucchini, garlic and mushrooms in a bowl and toss with the olive oil, oregano, salt and pepper. Place on a large baking sheet and roast for 20–30 minutes, or until the vegetables are tender and lightly browned. Remove the vegetables and reduce the oven temperature to 350°F (180°C).

Place the vegetables in a pot and mix in the diced and crushed tomatoes and tomato paste. Bring to a gentle simmer on the stovetop. Cover and cook, stirring occasionally, for 20 minutes. Season with salt and pepper. Combine the pesto, ricotta and eggs in a bowl, mixing well.

To assemble the lasagna, begin by spooning a little of the sauce into the bottom of a 9 x 13-inch (23 x 33-cm) baking dish. Top with 4 noodles. Spoon 1/3 of the remaining sauce over the noodles, and then add 1/3 of the mozzarella cheese. Top with 4 more noodles and then spread the ricotta mixture over top. Add 4 more noodles, and top them with 1/3 of the sauce and cheese. Repeat this step again and it's ready for the oven. Cover loosely with foil and bake for 40 minutes. Remove the foil and cook for 15–20 minutes more, or until brown and bubbling. Let rest for 10 minutes to allow the lasagna to set before slicing and serving.

VEAL-STUFFED PASTA SHELLS
with OLIVE TOMATO SAUCE

preparation time	·	30–40 minutes
cooking time	·	40–45 minutes
makes	·	4 servings

Jumbo pasta shells are a favourite because they present well and willingly accept just about any filling your heart desires. You'll find them alongside the other pastas sold in supermarkets.

THE SAUCE	2 Tbsp.	olive oil	25 mL
	1	medium onion, finely diced	1
	2	garlic cloves, crushed	2
	1 tsp. each	dried basil and dried oregano	5 mL
	1/2 cup	coarsely chopped black olives	125 mL
	1	28-oz. (796-mL) can tomato sauce	1
	2 Tbsp.	tomato paste	25 mL
	1 cup	red wine or beef stock	250 mL
	pinch	crushed chili flakes (optional)	pinch
	pinch	sugar	pinch
	to taste	salt and black pepper	to taste
THE STUFFED SHELLS	1 lb.	ground veal	500 g
	1	large egg	1
	1/4 cup	bread crumbs	50 mL
	2 Tbsp.	freshly grated Parmesan cheese	25 mL
	1 tsp. each	dried basil and dried oregano	5 mL
	2	garlic cloves, crushed	2
	to taste	salt and black pepper	to taste
	16–20	jumbo pasta shells, cooked as per package directions	16–20
	1 1/2 cups	grated mozzarella cheese	375 mL

THE SAUCE

Heat the oil in a pot over medium heat. And the onion and garlic cook until tender, about 3–4 minutes. Add the remaining sauce ingredients. Bring to a gentle simmer and cook, stirring occasionally, for 20 minutes.

THE STUFFED SHELLS

Preheat the oven to 375°F (190°C). Combine the veal, egg, bread crumbs, Parmesan cheese, basil, oregano, garlic, salt and pepper in a bowl. Place about 2 Tbsp (25 mL) of filling into each shell.

Spoon the sauce into a 9 x 13-inch (23 x 33-cm) casserole. Place the stuffed shells in the dish. Top each one with a little mozzarella cheese. Cover the dish loosely with foil and bake for 30 minutes. Remove the foil and bake for 10–15 minutes more, or until the tops of the shells are golden and the sauce is bubbling.

ERIC'S OPTIONS
You can use other ground meats, such as beef, turkey or chicken, instead of the veal. This dish can be prepared in advance, wrapped in plastic wrap, stored in the refrigerator for up to a day, and baked later. It also freezes well unbaked. Thaw in the refrigerator overnight before baking as directed.

BEEF and MACARONI CASSEROLE

preparation time · 20 minutes
cooking time · 30 minutes
makes · 6–8 servings

This homey casserole layers macaroni and cheese with a simple meat sauce. Choose your favourite store-bought pasta sauce to make the meat sauce.

ERIC'S OPTIONS
Substitute Italian-style cheeses, such as mozzarella, Asiago or provolone, for all or part of the Cheddar. This dish can be prepared in advance, wrapped in plastic wrap, stored in the refrigerator for up to a day, and baked later. It also freezes well unbaked. Thaw in the refrigerator overnight before baking as directed.

1 lb.	lean ground beef	500 g
1	medium onion, chopped	1
1	23-oz. (700-mL) jar of tomato-based pasta sauce	1
to taste	salt and freshly cracked black pepper	to taste
2¹/2 cups	macaroni	625 mL
2³/4 cups	milk	675 mL
¹/3 cup	all-purpose flour	75 mL
3 cups	grated Cheddar cheese	750 mL

Place the beef and onion in a pot over medium heat. Cook, stirring, until the meat is no longer pink and is entirely cooked through. Drain off any excess fat. Add the pasta sauce, season with salt and pepper and simmer gently for 20 minutes.

While the beef mixture simmers, bring a large pot of salted water to boil. Add the macaroni and cook until just tender. Place 2¹/2 cups (625 mL) of the milk into another pot and bring close to boiling. Place the remaining ¹/4 cup (50 mL) milk and flour in a small bowl and mix until lump-free. Quickly whisk the milk and flour mixture into the hot milk. Simmer gently, stirring occasionally, until the sauce thickens, about 5 minutes. (Be careful not to burn it.) Add 2 cups (500 mL) of the cheese and stir until well incorporated. Remove from the heat.

When the macaroni is cooked, drain it well and place it in a bowl. Mix in the cheese sauce and season with salt and pepper.

Preheat the oven to 350°F (180°C). Spoon the beef mixture into the bottom of a 9 x 13-inch (23 x 33-cm) casserole. Spoon the pasta mixture over top, carefully spreading it out to cover the meat sauce. Sprinkle with the remaining 1 cup (250 mL) cheese. Bake for 30 minutes, or until brown and bubbly.

GRILLED SIRLOIN on RICE NOODLES with GREEN ONIONS, GARLIC and GINGER

preparation time	·	20 minutes
cooking time	·	5 minutes
makes	·	4 servings

This brothy noodle dish can bring a little warmth on a cool winter day.

NOTE
Rice noodles, also sometimes called rice vermicelli, can be found in the Asian food aisle of your supermarket.

ERIC'S OPTIONS
Not a meat eater? Then replace the beef broth with a vegetable-based one and the beef with 2 cups (500 mL) of whole or thinly sliced vegetables, such as snow peas, carrots, red bell peppers, broccoli or baby corn. Stir-fry the vegetables, garlic, ginger and chili flakes in vegetable oil until just tender before mixing in the soy sauce. Top the noodles with the vegetables and pour in the broth.

2	garlic cloves, crushed	2
2 tsp.	grated fresh ginger	10 mL
2 Tbsp.	soy sauce	25 mL
1/4–1/2 tsp.	crushed chili flakes	1–2 mL
1 lb.	top sirloin steak	500 g
5 cups	canned or homemade beef broth	1.25 L
1 Tbsp.	sesame oil	15 mL
1	1/2-lb. (250-g) package rice noodles	1
6	green onions, chopped	6

Mix the garlic, ginger, soy sauce and crushed chili flakes in a bowl. Add the steak and turn to coat both sides with the marinade. Cover and marinate for 20 minutes. Grill the steak over high heat on a lightly oiled grill for 2–3 minutes per side. Remove and let rest for 5 minutes.

Bring a large pot of water to a boil for the noodles. Combine the broth and sesame oil in a separate pot and bring to a rapid boil. Cook the noodles in boiling water for 1 minute, or until just tender. Drain well and divide them among 4 large soup bowls. Thinly slice the beef and distribute on top of the noodles. Sprinkle with the green onions. Add the broth and serve.

Maple Whiskey-   60
Glazed Salmon

Baked Chilled Salmon Fillets   62
with Dill and Horseradish Sauce

Halibut and Spinach   64
Wrapped in Filo

Cedar Plank Salmon   66

Tuna Steaks Roasted with   67
Basil, Wine and Capers

Shrimp-Stuffed   68
Sole Fillets

Fish and Fresh   70
Vegetable Casserole

SIMPLY
SEAFOOD

CHAPTER FIVE

Baked Snapper with   71
Hoisin Sesame Glaze

Canadian-Style   72
Bouillabaisse

Beer and Chili   73
Steamed Mussels

Cornmeal-Crusted Crab Cakes   74
with Cayenne Mayonnaise

Grilled Prawns on Sweet,   76
Sour and Spicy Mangoes

MAPLE WHISKEY-
GLAZED SALMON

preparation time · 5 minutes
cooking time · 12–15 minutes
makes · 4 servings

Maple syrup, whiskey and salmon give this rich recipe a taste of Canada. Serve it with small new potatoes and seasonal vegetables.

ERIC'S OPTIONS
Feel free to adjust the level of sweetness or spiciness of the glaze. For example, if you prefer it less sweet, cut back a little on the maple syrup and add a little extra lemon. If you want it spicy, increase the amount of Dijon mustard. Bourbon can be used instead of whiskey. Trout fillets can replace the salmon.

4	6-oz. (175-g) salmon fillets or steaks	4
to taste	salt and freshly cracked black pepper	to taste
3 Tbsp.	maple syrup	45 mL
2 Tbsp.	whiskey	25 mL
1 Tbsp.	Dijon mustard	15 mL
1/2	lemon, juiced	1/2
2 tsp.	chopped fresh dill	10 mL
	dill sprigs and lemon wedges for garnish	

Preheat the oven to 425°F (220°C). Place the salmon in a shallow baking dish. Season with salt and pepper. Combine the maple syrup, whiskey, mustard, lemon juice and chopped dill in a bowl. Mix well and spoon over the fish. Bake for 12–15 minutes, or until the fish begins to flake slightly. Divide the salmon among 4 plates and spoon the pan juices over top. Garnish with dill sprigs and lemon wedges.

BUYING AND STORING FRESH FISH AND SHELLFISH

Fresh fish and shellfish should not smell "fishy." They should smell sweet and mildly of the sea or fresh water. Smelling the item in the store to check its quality is not something most people feel comfortable doing. However, you can ask the retailer when it came in — if it is more than a day old, it's likely past its prime. Appearance also tells a lot. Fresh fish will have firm flesh that glistens; it should not look soft and dull. The shells of mussels and clams should be shut tight, or should shut when gently tapped. If they don't shut, don't buy them. Purchase fresh fish or shellfish the day you intend to use it, if possible. If you need to store it for up to a day, remove it from its packaging, place it in a covered container, and store it in the coldest part of your refrigerator. To keep it super-chilled, set the container on a bowl of crushed ice.

BAKED CHILLED SALMON FILLETS
with DILL and HORSERADISH SAUCE

preparation time ·	15 minutes
cooking time ·	12–15 minutes
makes ·	8 servings

This recipe is ideal for summer gatherings. You can prepare the salmon and sauce in the morning when the kitchen is cool, refrigerate it, and have it ready to go when your guests arrive. The salmon pairs nicely with Roasted Pepper and Spinach Salad (page 24) or Spring Vegetable Salad (page 22).

ERIC'S OPTIONS
Use other fresh herbs, such as tarragon, chives and mint, or a combination of them, instead of the dill in this recipe. If you would like a spicier sauce, increase the amount of horse radish and Dijon mustard.

8	6-oz. (175-g) salmon fillets	8
1	lemon, juiced	1
2 Tbsp.	olive oil	25 mL
to taste	salt and freshly cracked black pepper	to taste
	cucumber slices, lemon wedges and dill sprigs	
3/4 cup	sour cream	175 mL
3/4 cup	mayonnaise	175 mL
2 Tbsp.	horseradish	25 mL
2 tsp.	chopped fresh dill	10 mL
2 tsp.	Dijon mustard	10 mL
to taste	salt, freshly cracked black pepper and lemon juice	to taste

Preheat the oven to 425°F (220°C). Place the salmon on a baking tray with sides. Drizzle with the lemon juice and oil. Season with salt and pepper. Cover and bake for 12–15 minutes. Remove from the oven, uncover and cool to room temperature.

Carefully transfer the salmon to a serving platter. Wrap and refrigerate until well chilled. Decorate the salmon with cucumber, lemon wedges and dill. Place the remaining ingredients in a bowl and mix well to combine. Serve the sauce alongside the salmon.

BAKING: THE SIMPLE WAY TO COOK FISH

Baking is the easiest and most versatile way to cook fish fillets or steaks. There's no flipping required; no worry that the fish is going to stick to the grill; and no fancy poaching liquid to create. All you require is a shallow-sided baking dish or tray that is large enough to allow the fish to be easily removed once cooked, but not so large that any liquid flavourings you add evaporate from the pan. Baking is one of the most flavourful ways to cook fish as the seasonings are in the pan, not simply brushed or poured on, allowing them to penetrate and enrich the flesh. Baked fish also cooks quickly; it usually takes about 12–15 minutes, depending on the thickness of the fish and the oven temperature.

HALIBUT and SPINACH WRAPPED in FILO

preparation time · 30 minutes
cooking time · 20 minutes
makes · 2 servings

Baking fish in filo pastry keeps it moist. It also creates a crispy exterior that's hard to resist, particularly when paired with the rich and creamy sauce featured in this dish.

THE FISH			
	1	10-oz (300-g) package frozen chopped spinach, thawed	1
	1 Tbsp.	butter	15 mL
	1	shallot, finely chopped	1
	1	garlic clove, crushed	1
	4	sheets filo pastry (see page 81)	4
	2–3 Tbsp.	melted butter	25–45 mL
	2	6-oz. (175-g) halibut fillets	2
	to taste	salt and freshly cracked black pepper	to taste

THE SAUCE			
	1 Tbsp.	butter	15 mL
	1	shallot, finely chopped	1
	2 Tbsp.	lemon juice	25 mL
	3/4 cup	whipping cream	175 mL
	2 Tbsp.	capers	25 mL
	1 Tbsp.	chopped chives	15 mL
	to taste	salt and freshly cracked black pepper	to taste

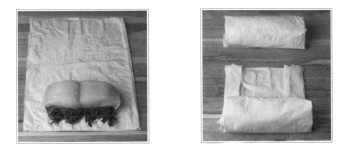

THE FISH

Squeeze as much moisture from the spinach as you can and set aside. Heat the 1 Tbsp. (15 mL) butter in a small skillet over medium heat. Add the shallot and garlic and cook until softened, about 1–2 minutes. Add the spinach and season with salt and pepper. Remove from the heat and set aside. Preheat the oven to 400°F (200°C).

Lay a sheet of filo pastry on your work surface. Brush lightly with melted butter. Top with another sheet and brush again. Repeat the process until all the sheets are used. Cut the stacked sheets in half. Divide the spinach mixture and place near the bottom centre of each sheet. Set the halibut on top of the spinach and season with salt and pepper. Fold the sides of the filo over to partially cover the halibut and then roll it up to form a package and seal the filling inside. (See photos on how to make a filo package). Place on a parchment-lined baking tray. Brush the tops with butter. Place on a middle rack in the oven for 20–25 minutes.

THE SAUCE

While the fish cooks, make the sauce. Melt the butter in a pot set over medium heat. Add the shallot and cook until softened, about 1–2 minutes. Add the lemon juice and continue cooking until it has almost all evaporated. Pour in the cream and cook until it thickens slightly. Add the capers and chives. Season with salt and pepper.

To serve, pour a pool of the sauce on 2 dinner plates. Cut each filo parcel in half at a slight angle. Arrange the pieces over the sauce.

ERIC'S OPTIONS

Other fish, such as salmon or cod, can replace the halibut. Instead of frozen chopped spinach, use a small bunch of fresh spinach, washed, stemmed, steamed, cooled, squeezed of excess moisture and chopped. If you are not fond of the taste of capers, omit them from the sauce.

CEDAR PLANK SALMON

preparation time · 10 minutes
cooking time · 15–20 minutes
makes · 4 servings

This salmon preparation is most often cooked on a barbecue, but it also works well in the oven. Either way, the cedar gives the salmon an inviting, slightly smoky taste. Serve it with corn on the cob, steamed new potatoes and green beans.

NOTE
Untreated cedar planks are available at many super-markets. You can also find the planks at lumber supply stores.

ERIC'S OPTIONS
Use an equal amount of maple syrup or honey instead of brown sugar. For pepper-crusted cedar plank salmon, coat the fish with a generous amount of coarsely cracked black pepper before cooking.

2 Tbsp.	olive oil	25 mL
1/2	lemon, juiced	1/2
1 Tbsp.	brown sugar	15 mL
1 Tbsp.	chopped fresh dill or parsley	15 mL
to taste	salt and black pepper	to taste
4	6-oz. (175-g) salmon fillets, skin on	4
	lemon slices	

Presoak an untreated cedar plank by submerging it in cold water for 2 hours. Place the oil, lemon juice, sugar, dill or parsley, salt and pepper in a bowl and mix well. Add the salmon and turn to coat. Marinate for 30 minutes.

Remove the plank from the water and dry the side the fish will be placed on. If you are using the oven, preheat it to 425°F (220°C). Place the fish on the plank and bake for 15–20 minutes, or until just cooked through. If using the barbecue, preheat it to medium-high. If you have a two-burner barbecue, turn one side off and lower the other to medium-low. Set the fish on the plank and place on the unlit side of the barbecue. (If you have a one-burner barbecue, set to its lowest setting.) Close the lid and cook for 15–20 minutes, or until the fish is cooked through. Keep a spray bottle handy just in case the board ignites on the bottom. Set the plank on a serving tray and garnish with lemon slices.

TUNA STEAKS ROASTED with BASIL, WINE and CAPERS

preparation time · 5 minutes
cooking time · 8 – 10 minutes
makes · 4 servings

This recipe is a fast and delicious way to enjoy the rich, meaty flavour of tuna. Complete the meal with a simple pasta dish, sliced tomatoes and olives.

ERIC'S OPTIONS
Other firm-fleshed fish steaks, such as swordfish or marlin, could be used instead of tuna. If you are not fond of capers, try substituting an equal amount of chopped sun-dried tomatoes.

4	5-oz. (150-g) fresh or frozen (thawed) tuna steaks	4
3 Tbsp.	olive oil	45 mL
1/2	lemon, juiced	1/2
1/4 cup	dry white wine	50 mL
3 Tbsp.	capers	45 mL
3	garlic cloves, thickly sliced	3
2 Tbsp.	chopped fresh basil	25 mL
to taste	salt and freshly cracked black pepper	to taste

Preheat the oven to 425°F (220°C). Place the tuna in a shallow baking dish. Mix the remaining ingredients in a bowl and pour the mixture over the tuna. Bake for 8–10 minutes. Do not overcook. Place the tuna on dinner plates and spoon the pan juices over top.

SHRIMP-STUFFED
SOLE FILLETS

preparation time · 20 minutes
cooking time · 15–20 minutes
makes · 2 servings

This elegant fish dish for 2 can be put together quite quickly. Complement it with baby potatoes and tiny carrots with their tops, fiddleheads, or small asparagus spears.

THE FILLING	5 oz.	small cooked shrimp (see page 77), coarsely chopped	150 g
	1 tsp.	chopped fresh dill	5 mL
	1	large egg white	1
	1	garlic clove, crushed	1
	1/4 cup	bread crumbs	50 mL
	to taste	salt, freshly cracked black pepper and lemon juice	to taste
THE FISH	4	sole fillets, totalling 3/4 lb. (375 g)	4
	to taste	salt and black pepper	to taste
	2 Tbsp.	olive oil	25 mL
	1 tsp.	chopped fresh dill	5 mL
	1	garlic clove, crushed	1
	1/4 cup	white wine	50 mL
		dill sprigs and lemon wedges	

THE FILLING
Place the filling ingredients in a bowl and mix well.

THE FISH
Preheat the oven to 375°F (190°C). Season the sole fillets with salt and pepper and lay them flat on a work surface. Divide and mound the filling at the narrow end of each fillet. Roll the fillets up tight and place in a small baking dish. (The fish can be prepared to this point several hours before cooking and stored in the refrigerator.) Combine the oil, chopped dill, garlic and wine in a small bowl. Pour over the fish. Cover with foil and bake for 15–20 minutes, or until the fish begins to slightly flake and turn opaque. To serve, place 2 pieces of sole on each plate and spoon the pan juices over top. Garnish with dill and lemon.

ERIC'S OPTIONS
Use crabmeat in the filling instead of shrimp. Use other thin, boneless fish fillets suitable for rolling, such as flounder or plaice, instead of sole.

FISH and FRESH VEGETABLE CASSEROLE

preparation time · 20 minutes
cooking time · 15 minutes
makes · 2 servings

A quick and easy casserole that provides a tasty, healthy dinner for two all in one pan.

ERIC'S OPTIONS
Try baking cooked and cooled green beans, asparagus spears or cauliflower alongside the fish. To spice the dish up a bit, sprinkle the fish and vegetables before baking with Cajun spice or your favourite seafood spice blend.

8–12	small new potatoes, halved	8–12
1	medium carrot, thickly sliced	1
12–18	snow or snap peas, trimmed	12–18
2 Tbsp.	olive oil or melted butter	25 mL
2	5- to 6-oz. (150- to 175-g) fish fillets, such as snapper, salmon or halibut	2
1/2	lemon, juiced	1/2
to taste	salt and freshly cracked black pepper	to taste
1 Tbsp.	chopped fresh parsley or other fresh herb	15 mL

Preheat the oven to 425°F (220°C). Place the potatoes and carrots in a pot and cover with cold water. Bring to a boil and cook until firm-tender. Add the peas and cook just until they turn bright green. Drain the vegetables, immerse in cold water to cool, then drain again.

Brush a shallow baking dish with 1 Tbsp. (15 mL) of the olive oil or melted butter. Place the fish in the casserole and surround with the cooked vegetables. Drizzle with the remaining oil or butter, sprinkle with lemon juice, and season with salt and pepper. Bake for 15 minutes, or until the fish is opaque and just begins to flake. Sprinkle with parsley and serve.

BAKED SNAPPER with HOISIN SESAME GLAZE

preparation time · 10 minutes
cooking time · 12–15 minutes
makes · 4 servings

The snapper in this quick-cooking dish is deliciously flavoured with a classic Asian-style taste combination of hot, sour and sweet. To round out the meal, serve it with steamed rice or noodles and stir-fried vegetables.

NOTE
Hoisin sauce and Asian-style chili sauce can be found in the Asian food aisle of your local supermarket.

ERIC'S OPTIONS
Use halibut, swordfish or salmon fillets instead of snapper. For a salty and more pungent taste, substitute black bean sauce for the hoisin.

4	6-oz. (175-g) snapper fillets	4
1/3 cup	hoisin sauce	75 mL
2 Tbsp.	rice wine vinegar	25 mL
1 Tbsp.	honey, or to taste	15 mL
2	garlic cloves, chopped	2
2 tsp.	grated fresh ginger	10 mL
1 tsp.	Asian-style hot sauce	5 mL
2 Tbsp.	sesame seeds	25 mL
2	finely chopped green onions	2

Preheat the oven to 425°F (220°C). Place the snapper in a shallow, lightly oiled baking dish. Combine the hoisin, vinegar, honey, garlic, ginger and hot sauce in a bowl, mixing well. Spoon the glaze over the fish. Sprinkle with sesame seeds. Bake for 12–15 minutes, or until the fish begins to slightly flake. Divide the fish among 4 plates, spoon the pan juices over top and sprinkle with green onions.

CANADIAN-STYLE BOUILLABAISSE

preparation time · 20 minutes
cooking time · 18–20 minutes
makes · 4 servings

I call this "Canadian-style" bouillabaisse because the seafood in it comes from our oceans. Serve it with thin slices of lightly toasted baguette and Quick Rouille (page 143).

ERIC'S OPTIONS
If you're feeling decadent, add whole, cooked lobster cut into smaller pieces along with the mussels and clams.

2 Tbsp.	olive oil	25 mL
2	garlic cloves, chopped	2
1	large onion, diced	1
4	ripe medium tomatoes, seeded and chopped	4
1 cup	dry white wine	250 mL
3 1/2 cups	chicken, vegetable or fish stock	875 mL
1/2 tsp.	fennel seeds	2 mL
pinch	saffron threads	pinch
1/2 lb	halibut or salmon fillets, cubed	250 g
2–3 Tbsp.	chopped fresh tarragon or parsley	25–45 mL
to taste	salt and black pepper	to taste
16 each	mussels and clams	16 each
8	Digby scallops, halved	8
1/4 lb.	small cooked shrimp (see page 77)	125 g

Heat the oil in a large, wide pot over medium heat. Add the garlic and onion and cook until tender, about 2–3 minutes. Add the tomatoes, wine, stock, fennel and saffron. Bring to a gentle simmer and cook for 10 minutes. Add the halibut or salmon and cook for 2 minutes. Add the remaining ingredients, cover, and cook until the clams and mussels open, about 4–5 minutes. Discard any clams that do not open. Divide the seafood among heated bowls and ladle the broth over top.

BEER and CHILI
STEAMED MUSSELS

preparation time	·	5 minutes
cooking time	·	3–5 minutes
makes	·	2 servings

Ice cold lager, naturally, is the perfect drink to pair with these spicy, beer-steamed mussels. For a more rounded meal, serve the mussels on steamed rice or Asian-style noodles and accompany with steamed or stir-fried vegetables.

ERIC'S OPTIONS
Use clams instead of mussels.

36	fresh mussels	36
1 Tbsp.	vegctable oil	15 mL
2	garlic cloves, chopped	2
2 tsp.	chopped fresh ginger	10 mL
2–3 tsp.	Asian-style chili sauce, or to taste	10–15 mL
1/2 cup	lager	125 mL
2 Tbsp.	soy sauce	25 mL
2 Tbsp.	chopped green onions	25 mL

Rinse the mussels in cold water, pull away any beard-like material from their shells, and then drain well. Heat the oil in a pot set over medium-high heat. Add the garlic, ginger and chili sauce and cook until fragrant, about 30 seconds. Add the lager and soy sauce and bring to a boil. Add the mussels, cover the pot and cook just until the mussels open. Transfer the mussels to 2 bowls, discarding any that are not open. Spoon the cooking liquid over top and sprinkle with green onions.

CORNMEAL-CRUSTED CRAB CAKES
with CAYENNE MAYONNAISE

preparation time · 20 minutes
cooking time · 6–8 minutes
makes · 8 crab cakes—serves 4 as a starter or light entrée

Fresh, frozen or canned crabmeat can be used in this recipe. When using frozen and canned, ensure you squeeze out as much moisture as you as can, otherwise your crab cakes will have a watered-down taste. A simple green salad goes well with these crab cakes.

ERIC'S OPTIONS
Bread or cracker crumbs can replace the cornmeal. For spicier crab cakes, add 1 Tbsp. (15 mL) finely chopped fresh jalapeño pepper to the mix before shaping into cakes.

1/2 cup	mayonnaise	125 mL
to taste	cayenne, salt and lime juice	to taste
2 cups	crabmeat	500 mL
1	large egg, beaten	1
2 Tbsp.	all-purpose flour	25 mL
3 Tbsp.	mayonnaise	45 mL
3	green onions, finely chopped	3
1/4 cup	very finely chopped red bell pepper	50 mL
2 Tbsp.	chopped fresh cilantro or parsley	25 mL
1/2	lime, juiced	1/2
to taste	salt and hot pepper sauce	to taste
1 cup	cornmeal	250 mL
3 Tbsp.	vegetable oil	45 mL
	lime wedges and cilantro or parsley sprigs	

Place the ½ cup (125 mL) of mayonnaise, cayenne, salt and lime juice in a bowl and mix well to combine. Cover and set aside in the refrigerator.

Line a tray with plastic wrap or parchment paper. Place the crabmeat, egg, flour, 3 Tbsp. (45 mL) of mayonnaise, onions, bell pepper, cilantro or parsley, lime juice, salt and hot pepper sauce in a bowl and mix well to combine. (The mixture will be very moist, which will ensure moist crab cakes.) Place the cornmeal in a shallow dish. Dampen your hands lightly with water and shape ¼ cup (50 mL) of the crab mixture into a ball. Set it on the cornmeal. Sprinkle the top and sides with cornmeal and then gently form into a cake about 3 inches (8 cm) wide and ½ inch (1 cm) thick. Place on the prepared tray. Repeat with the remaining crab mixture. You should get 8 crab cakes.

Heat the oil in a large, preferably non-stick skillet over medium heat. Cook the crab cakes for 3–4 minutes per side. Drain the crab cakes on paper towels and then place on serving plates. Serve with a dollop of the flavoured mayonnaise and garnish with lime wedges and cilantro or parsley sprigs.

EQUIVALENTS FOR 2 CUPS (500 ML) OF CRABMEAT

- about 300 g of fresh, cooked crabmeat, flaked
- 2 4¼-oz. (120-g) cans, of crabmeat with leg and body meat, drained and squeezed of excess moisture and flaked
- 14 oz. (400 g) of frozen crab meat with leg and body meat, thawed, drained and squeezed of excess moisture and flaked

GRILLED PRAWNS on SWEET, SOUR and SPICY MANGOES

preparation time · 20 minutes
cooking time · 4 minutes
makes · 4 servings

Here's a tropical-tasting dish that can be served simply as an appetizer or light lunch, or with steamed jasmine rice, curried vegetables and pappadums for a more filling, Indian-style lunch or dinner.

THE MANGOES	2 Tbsp.	brown sugar	25 mL
	2	limes, juiced	2
	pinch	crushed chili flakes	pinch
	1/2 cup	finely chopped red onion	125 mL
	2 Tbsp.	chopped fresh mint	25 mL
	2 Tbsp.	chopped cilantro	25 mL
	2	ripe medium mangoes, peeled and thinly sliced	2
	pinch	salt	pinch
THE PRAWNS	2 Tbsp.	olive oil	25 mL
	pinch	crushed chili flakes	pinch
	1 tsp.	ground cumin	5 mL
	1 tsp.	chili powder	5 mL
	1/2 tsp.	salt	2 mL
	20–24	large prawns, peeled leaving tail portion intact	20–24
		lime wedges and mint or cilantro sprigs	

THE MANGOES

Mix the sugar and lime juice in a large bowl until the sugar is dissolved. Mix in the chili flakes, onion, mint and cilantro. Add the mangoes, toss gently, and set aside at room temperature.

THE PRAWNS

Combine the oil, chili flakes, cumin, chili powder and salt in a bowl large enough to hold the prawns. Toss the prawns in the mixture and marinate 20–30 minutes.

Grill the prawns over medium-high heat for 2 minutes per side, or until just cooked through. To serve, gently toss the mangoes again and arrange them on 4 plates. Arrange the prawns on top of the mangoes. Garnish with lime wedges and mint or cilantro sprigs.

SHRIMP AND PRAWNS

When is a shrimp a prawn or a prawn a shrimp? It depends on where you make your home. On the west coast of British Columbia, where I live, medium to large shrimp are called prawns. The term shrimp is reserved for the small, cooked shellfish used for salads and sandwiches. However, east of the Rocky Mountains, all these crustaceans, large or small, are most often called shrimp.

Regardless of what you call them (I'll use shrimp the rest of the way), the way they are priced and sold is the same. Shrimp are priced and categorized according to size; this is determined by the count, or number per pound (once the head is removed). Jumbo shrimp are 11–15 per pound; extra-large, 16–20; large, 21–30; medium, 31–35; and small, 36–45. Although there are variances in texture and flavour, the different sizes can generally be substituted for one another.

Shrimp can be bought raw or cooked, shelled or unshelled, and fresh or frozen. The raw shrimp found in the fresh seafood case at supermarkets, unless it is from nearby waters, has been frozen and then thawed.

Deveining (removing the grey-black vein from the back of raw or cooked shrimp) before eating or cooking shrimp is a matter of personal preference. Small and medium shrimp do not need deveining except for aesthetic purposes. However, because the intestinal vein of larger shrimp contains grit, I prefer to remove it.

ERIC'S OPTIONS
Use large scallops instead of prawns. Grill for a similar length of time. Replace the mango with half a small pineapple, cored, quartered and thinly sliced.

VEGETARIAN ENTRÉES

Asparagus, Roasted Pepper
and Mushroom Strudel — 80

Stuffed Baked Potatoes with
Aged Cheddar and Asparagus — 82

Portobello Mushroom Burgers
with Lemon Basil Mayonnaise — 84

Creole-Style
Stuffed Eggplant — 85

Exotic Mushroom
Risotto — 86

Vegetarian
Tourtière — 88

Curried Vegetable
Stew — 90

CHAPTER SIX

ASPARAGUS, ROASTED PEPPER and MUSHROOM STRUDEL

preparation time	·	30–40 minutes
cooking time	·	25–30 minutes
makes	·	4–6 servings

Serve this savoury strudel when you're looking for an attractive, non-meat dish to anchor a celebratory meal. I served it at Easter one year and it was a hit. Tzatziki (page 144) and Spring Vegetable Salad (page 22) are good accompaniments.

NOTE
You can use store-bought or home-made roasted red peppers (see page 13) in this dish.

ERIC'S OPTIONS
If asparagus is unavailable, use 2–2½ cups (500–625 mL) of small, blanched broccoli florets instead.

2 Tbsp.	olive oil	25 mL
1 lb.	brown or white mushrooms, sliced	500 g
3	green onions, finely chopped	3
¼ cup	bread crumbs	50 mL
1	large egg, beaten	1
2	garlic cloves, crushed	2
to taste	salt and freshly cracked black pepper	to taste
5	sheets of filo pastry (see next page)	5
¼ cup	melted butter or olive oil	50 mL
2 lbs.	asparagus, trimmed and blanched (see page 83)	1 kg
to taste	salt and freshly cracked black pepper	to taste
⅓ cup	freshly grated Parmesan cheese	75 mL
3	roasted red peppers, halved and patted dry	3

Preheat the oven to 375°F (190°C). Heat the oil in a skillet over medium-high heat. Add the mushrooms and cook until they are tender and their moisture has evaporated. Cool the mushrooms to room temperature. Mix with the onions, bread crumbs, egg, garlic and salt and pepper.

Lay a sheet of filo pastry on a non-stick or parchment-lined baking tray and brush with butter or oil. Top with another sheet and brush again. Repeat the process until all the sheets are used. Arrange the asparagus in the middle of the bottom third of the pastry. (See photos on how to fill and fold filo.) Sprinkle with salt, pepper and the Parmesan cheese. Top with the roasted peppers and then the mushroom mixture. Fold the sides of the pastry slightly over the filling and carefully fold the filling over and enclose in the pastry. Brush the top with a little melted butter or oil. Make small cuts, about 2 inches (5 cm) apart, in the top of the pastry to make it easier to cut when baked. Bake for 25–30 minutes. Let rest for 10 minutes before slicing with a sharp, serrated knife.

HANDLING AND STORING FILO PASTRY

Filo (also called phyllo) pastry is sold frozen in most supermarkets. Thaw at room temperature for 3–4 hours before using. Filo pastry is delicate. Make sure you have a clear, large work space to move and fold it without tearing it. Carefully unfold the sheets and remove the amount you need. Refold the remaining sheets and tightly seal the package. Refrigerate any unused sheets for 2–3 weeks. Filo pastry can also be refrozen. Divide it into packages that contain the number of sheets you will most likely use each time.

STUFFED BAKED POTATOES with AGED CHEDDAR and ASPARAGUS

preparation time · 30 minutes
cooking time · 75–90 minutes
makes · 4 servings

These hearty stuffed potatoes can be a dinner in themselves when served with Light and Delicious Caesar Salad (page 20). As a side dish, they go nicely with grilled steaks, chicken and fish, or with Pork Side Ribs with Chipotle Barbecue Sauce (page 134).

ERIC'S OPTIONS
Use sharp-tasting cheese, such as Swiss or aged Gouda, instead of Cheddar.

4	large baking potatoes, scrubbed well	4
3 Tbsp.	melted butter	45 mL
3/4 cup	buttermilk	175 mL
1 cup	grated aged Cheddar cheese	250 mL
8	asparagus spears, trimmed, blanched and thinly sliced	8
to taste	salt and freshly cracked black pepper	to taste
	chopped chives or green onions	

Preheat the oven to 425°F (220°C). Prick each potato a few times with a fork. Bake the potatoes until very tender, about 50–60 minutes. Set aside until cool enough to handle. Cut off the top one-third of each potato.

Carefully scoop out as much of the flesh as you can and place in a bowl. Place the potato shells in a baking dish. Mash the potatoes until smooth. Mix in the butter and buttermilk. Whip as hard as you can to increase the volume of the potatoes. Mix in 2/3 of the cheese, the sliced asparagus, salt and pepper. Spoon the mixture into the potato shells. Top with the remaining 1/3 cheese. Bake until golden brown, about 25–30 minutes. Garnish potatoes with chopped chives or green onions just before serving.

BLANCHING VEGETABLES

Vegetables are blanched by plunging them into boiling water and cooking them — usually — to firm-tender. The length of time it takes depends on the type of vegetable and whether it will be cooked afterward. In general, quick-cooking vegetables, such as asparagus, green beans, snow peas and broccoli florets, will take 1–2 minutes; firmer vegetables, such as Brussels sprouts, will take 5–6. Once blanched, the vegetables are quickly chilled in ice water to stop the cooking process and set their colour. Drain well before using.

PORTOBELLO MUSHROOM BURGERS
with LEMON BASIL MAYONNAISE

preparation time · 10 minutes
cooking time · 4–6 minutes
makes · 4 servings

The meaty taste and large, round shape of portobellos make them perfect for burgers. Try these burgers with Roasted New Potatoes with Lemon and Dijon (page 152).

ERIC'S OPTIONS
Add slices of Italian-style cheese, such as mozzarella or provolone, for a deluxe burger.

4	portobello mushrooms, 4–5 inches (10–12 cm) in diameter	4
2 Tbsp.	olive oil	25 mL
1/2 cup	mayonnaise	125 mL
3 Tbsp.	chopped fresh basil	45 mL
to taste	salt, fresh cracked black pepper and lemon juice	to taste
4	burger buns	4
4	lettuce leaves	4
4–8	thin slices ripe tomato	4–8
4–8	thin slices onion	4–8

Remove the stems from the mushrooms and discard or save for soup stock. Brush the mushrooms with oil and sprinkle with salt and pepper. Grill or pan-fry in a non-stick grill pan or skillet over medium-high heat for 2–3 minutes per side, or until the mushroom are just tender. Place the mayonnaise, basil, salt, pepper and lemon juice in a bowl and mix well to combine. Spread the flavoured mayonnaise on the buns, top each with a mushroom and some lettuce, tomato and onion, and serve.

CREOLE-STYLE STUFFED EGGPLANT

preparation time · 30–40 minutes
cooking time · 40–45 minutes
makes · 4 servings

Serve steamed rice and a green salad with this satisfying main-course vegetarian dish.

ERIC'S OPTIONS
If you don't have fresh tomatoes on hand, you can use an equal amount of diced canned tomatoes. If you don't have fresh herbs, substitute 2 tsp. (10 mL) of dried herbs for 2 Tbsp. (25 mL) fresh. Add the dried herbs when you add the tomatoes.

2 Tbsp.	olive oil	25 mL
1	medium onion, finely chopped	1
2	celery ribs, finely chopped	2
1	medium green bell pepper, finely chopped	1
2	garlic cloves, crushed	2
2	medium eggplants, 1 lb. (500 g) each	2
	lemon juice	
1/2 tsp.	cayenne pepper, or to taste	2 mL
1 1/2 cups	chopped fresh tomatoes	375 mL
2 Tbsp.	chopped fresh basil or oregano	25 mL
2 Tbsp.	chopped fresh parsley	25 mL
1/2 cup	bread crumbs	125 mL
to taste	salt and black pepper	to taste
1 1/2 cups	grated Monterey Jack cheese	375 mL

Preheat the oven to 375°F (190°C). Heat the oil in a large skillet over medium heat. Add the onion, celery, green pepper and garlic and cook until tender, about 4–5 minutes. Stem the eggplants and cut in half lengthwise. With a sharp knife score the flesh side. Spoon out pulp, leaving a shell about 1/4 inch (5 mm) thick. Set them in a lightly oiled baking dish, brush the flesh with a little lemon juice, and set aside. Chop the pulp and add it to the skillet with the cayenne and tomatoes. Add just enough water to keep the mixture moist, and gently simmer until the eggplant is tender. Stir in the herbs, bread crumbs, salt and pepper. Stuff the eggplant shells with the mixture and top with the cheese. Bake for 30–40 minutes, until the shells are tender but not collapsed and the top is golden brown.

EXOTIC MUSHROOM RISOTTO

preparation time · 20 minutes
cooking time · 25–30 minutes
makes · 4 servings as a main course, 6 as a side dish

If you'd like to sample some of the more interesting-looking fresh mushrooms available these days, this dish is a good choice. Brown (cremini), oyster, portobello, chanterelle and morel are some of the mushrooms you can use in this risotto. I used a mix of the first three. If serving the risotto as a main course, just add some crusty Italian bread and a salad of mixed baby greens dressed with simple vinaigrette to complete the meal. As a side dish, try it with Roast Chicken Scented with Lemon, Garlic and Rosemary (page 92).

NOTE
Arborio, Canaroli, Baldo and Vialone Nano are some of the varieties of stubby, short-grained rice suitable for risotto. Some companies simply label rice suitable for risotto as risotto or Italian-style rice.

6 cups	lightly salted chicken or vegetable stock	1.5 L
3 Tbsp.	butter or olive oil	45 mL
1	medium onion, finely chopped	1
2–3	garlic cloves, finely chopped	2–3
1 1/2 cups	risotto rice	375 mL
1/2 cup	white wine	125 mL
2 Tbsp.	butter or olive oil	25 mL
1 lb.	assorted fresh mushrooms, sliced	500 g
to taste	salt and freshly cracked black pepper	to taste
2 Tbsp.	chopped Italian parsley	25 mL
1/2 cup	freshly grated Parmigiano-Reggiano cheese	125 mL

Place the stock in a pot and bring to a gentle simmer. Heat the 3 Tbsp. (45 mL) of butter or oil in another pot over medium heat. Add the onion and garlic and cook, stirring, until tender, about 2–3 minutes. Add the rice and cook, stirring, for 3–4 minutes, until the rice has a slightly nutty, toasted aroma. Add the wine, adjust the heat so the mixture gently simmers, and cook until the wine is almost fully absorbed. Add 1 cup (250 mL) of the hot stock, stirring and cooking until it is almost fully absorbed. Add the remaining stock 1/2 cup (125 mL) at a time, cooking and stirring until the liquid is almost absorbed each time. You may not need all the stock.

While the rice is cooking, heat the remaining 2 Tbsp. (25 mL) butter or oil in a large skillet over medium-high heat. Add the mushrooms and cook until they are tender and the moisture is gone. Season with salt and pepper and set aside.

When the rice is tender and creamy, remove it from the heat and stir in the parsley, cheese and mushrooms. Taste for seasoning and adjust, if necessary. Top with additional cheese at the table, if desired.

ERIC'S OPTIONS
To make the risotto even richer, drizzle it with a little truffle oil at the table. Truffle oil, which is made by infusing good-quality olive oil with the flavour of white or black truffles, is available at Italian-style markets and most fancy food stores.

VEGETARIAN
TOURTIÈRE

preparation time	·	30 minutes
cooking time	·	45–50 minutes
makes	·	6–8 servings

Pickled beets, pickles, mustard pickles, chutneys and relishes — homemade if you have them — are items that go great with the tourtière. You can use a store-bought or homemade pie crust — see Pastry for a Double Crust Pie (page 173).

NOTE
Yves Veggie Ground Round Original, sold at most supermarkets, looks and tastes similar to beef but is made with ingredients such as soy and wheat protein. If you cannot find it, substitute any similar vegetarian product sold in your area.

2 Tbsp.	vegetable oil	25 mL
1	medium onion, finely diced	1
2	garlic cloves, chopped	2
2	3/4-lb. (375-g) pouches Yves Veggie Ground Round Original	2
2 Tbsp.	all-purpose flour	25 mL
1 1/4 cups	vegetable stock	300 mL
1 1/4 cups	water	300 mL
1 tsp.	dried thyme	5 mL
1/2 tsp.	ground cloves	2 mL
1 1/2 tsp.	ground cinnamon	7.5 mL
1 cup	small potato cubes, cooked until just tender	250 mL
1 Tbsp.	chopped fresh parsley	15 mL
to taste	salt and freshly cracked black pepper	to taste
1	9-inch (23-cm) deep-dish double crust pie shell	1
	oil or beaten egg	

Heat the oil in a pot over medium heat. Add the onion and garlic and cook until tender, about 3–4 minutes. Add the Veggie Ground Round and stir to break it up. Mix in the flour until well combined. Pour in the stock and water. Add the thyme, cloves and cinnamon. Cook, stirring, until the liquid has almost evaporated. Stir in the potatoes, parsley, salt and pepper. Remove from the heat, cool to room temperature and refrigerate overnight.

Preheat the oven to 425°F (220°C). Place the filling in the bottom crust. Brush the sides with a little water or beaten egg. Place the top crust on and crimp the edges to seal. Cut out a small circle in the centre to allow steam to escape. Decorate the top of the tourtière with extra pastry if desired. Brush the top crust with a little oil or beaten egg. Bake for 20 minutes, then reduce the heat to 350°F (180°C) and bake 25–30 minutes more. Allow the tourtière to set for about 10 minutes before slicing.

ERIC'S OPTIONS
Allowing the filling to sit in the refrigerator overnight gives the flavours a chance to meld and become richer. However, if time is short, you can skip this step and assemble and bake the tourtière as soon as the filling has cooled. Unbaked tourtière freezes well. Thaw in the refrigerator overnight before baking.

CURRIED VEGETABLE STEW

preparation time · 20 minutes
cooking time · 20 minutes
makes · 3–4 servings

You can tailor this stew to the level of heat you like simply by choosing mild, medium or hot curry paste. Serve with chutney, yogurt, steamed rice and pappadums or naan.

NOTE
Curry paste is sold at most supermarkets and Asian-style markets.

ERIC'S OPTIONS
Just about any vegetable will work in this curry. Feel free to substitute any that you have on hand or that appeal to you more. Before cooking, evaluate their cooking time to decide when they should be added during the cooking process.

2 Tbsp.	vegetable oil	25 mL
1	large red bell pepper, seeded and cubed	1
1	medium onion, halved and thinly sliced	1
2	garlic cloves, finely chopped	2
1 Tbsp.	chopped fresh ginger	15 mL
2 Tbsp.	curry paste	25 mL
2	medium carrots, cut into 1/2-inch-thick (1-cm) coins	2
1	14-oz. (398-mL) can coconut milk	1
1/2 cup	vegetable stock	125 mL
1/2 lb.	green beans, trimmed and cut into 1-inch (2.5-cm) pieces	250 g
1/2	small head cauliflower, cut into small florets	1/2
1/4 cup	chopped cilantro	50 mL
to taste	salt	to taste

Heat the oil in a wide pot over medium-high heat. Add the red pepper and onion and cook until just tender, about 3–4 minutes. Stir in the garlic, ginger and curry paste and cook 2 minutes more. Stir in the carrots, coconut milk and stock. Reduce the heat to a gentle simmer and cook, stirring occasionally, until the carrots are almost tender, about 10 minutes. Add the green beans and cauliflower and cook until the sauce thickens slightly and the vegetables are tender. Add more stock if the curry becomes too thick before the vegetables are cooked. Stir in the cilantro and salt.

Roast Chicken Scented with Lemon, Garlic and Rosemary 92

Spinach and Raisin–Stuffed Chicken Breasts 94

Grilled Chicken with Summer Berries and Goat Cheese 96

Honey and Citrus–Glazed Chicken Breast 97

Cornmeal-Crusted Chicken Legs 98

Garlic-Stuffed Chicken Legs with Pan Gravy 99

Teriyaki Chicken and Vegetable Stir-Fry 100

One-Pan Mediterranean-Style Chicken Dinner 102

Quick and Easy Chicken Enchiladas 103

CHICKEN AND OTHER FINE TASTING FOWL

CHAPTER SEVEN

Sage and Mustard-Crusted Cornish Game Hen 104

Cornish Game Hens with Orange, Rosemary and Cranberry Glaze 105

Turkey Shepherd's Pie with Yukon Gold Mashed Potatoes 106

Heavenly Spiced Turkey and Vegetable Kebabs 108

Spice-Roasted Duck with Hoisin Glaze 110

ROAST CHICKEN SCENTED with LEMON, GARLIC and ROSEMARY

preparation time	·	20 minutes
cooking time	·	1 3/4–2 hours
makes	·	4 servings

Rosemary, lemon and garlic are three of my favourite flavourings, and they go beautifully with my family's first choice for Sunday dinner — roast chicken. To ensure the entire bird is infused with these flavours, I place them on the skin, under the skin and inside the cavity.

ERIC'S OPTIONS
If you would like gravy, remove the fat from the pan drippings, add 3 cups (750 mL) of chicken stock and bring to a boil. Mix 1/4 cup (50 mL) of all-purpose flour with 1/2 cup (125 mL) of chicken stock until smooth. Slowly whisk into the boiling stock and simmer until the gravy thickens.

1	4-lb. (2-kg) roasting chicken	1
8	garlic cloves, thinly sliced	8
1	lemon	1
2	medium onions, quartered	2
	fresh rosemary sprigs	
2 Tbsp.	olive oil	25 mL
1–2 Tbsp.	chopped fresh rosemary	15–25 mL
to taste	salt and freshly cracked black pepper	to taste

Preheat the oven to 350°F (180°C). Rinse the chicken in cold water and pat dry. Carefully lift up the skin at the top of the breast and slide half of the garlic slices underneath, pushing the pieces into different spots around the chicken. Place the chicken in a roasting pan.

Zest and juice the lemon and place in a small bowl. Set aside. Cut the remains of the lemon into chunks. Stuff the lemon chunks, onions, remaining garlic and a few rosemary sprigs into the cavity of the chicken. Tie the legs together. Add the oil and chopped rosemary to the lemon juice and zest. Mix well and brush the mixture all over the chicken. Season with salt and pepper. Roast 1 3/4–2 hours, or until cooked through and the temperature in the deepest part of the thigh registers 100°F (82°C) on a meat thermometer. Baste occasionally with the pan juices during cooking.

Remove the chicken from the pan and let it rest 10–15 minutes before carving.

An accompaniment of roasted vegetables is an economical and efficient use of oven space. Prepare 2 quartered medium onions, 4–6 quartered medium potatoes, and 2 thickly sliced carrots, celery ribs and parsnips. Arrange in a lightly buttered or oiled casserole dish and pour in 1 cup (250 mL) of chicken stock. Season with salt and pepper. Roast in a 350°F (180°C) oven for 1 hour, or until the vegetables are tender, brushing with stock from the pan occasionally. For added colour, sprinkle in 1 cup (250 mL) of thawed, frozen peas 10 minutes before other the vegetables are done.

SPINACH and RAISIN–STUFFED CHICKEN BREASTS

preparation time	·	30 minutes
cooking time	·	20–25 minutes
makes	·	4 servings

The sweetness of raisins and brown sugar, acidity of tomatoes and citrus, earthiness of spinach, and richness of pine nuts gives plain old chicken breasts a colourful, Mediterranean-style look and taste. Serve this dish with Orzo Baked with Green Onions and Parmesan (page 145).

ERIC'S OPTIONS
A small bunch of fresh spinach, washed, stemmed, steamed, cooled, squeezed of excess moisture and chopped, could replace the frozen spinach. Try other unsalted nuts, such as slivered almonds or coarsely chopped pistachios, instead of the pine nuts. Similar sized boneless, skinless turkey cutlets could be used instead of the chicken.

4	6-oz. (175-g) boneless, skinless chicken breasts	4
1/3 cup	raisins	75 mL
3 Tbsp.	pine nuts	45 mL
1	large egg, beaten	1
1	10-oz (300-g) package frozen, chopped spinach, thawed, moisture squeezed out	1
to taste	salt and freshly cracked black pepper	to taste
1 Tbsp.	olive oil	15 mL
1	14-oz. (398-mL) can tomato sauce	1
1 Tbsp.	brown sugar	15 mL
2 Tbsp.	lemon juice	25 mL
1/4 cup	orange juice	50 mL
to taste	salt and freshly cracked black pepper	to taste
2 Tbsp.	chopped fresh mint or basil	25 mL

Preheat the oven to 425°F (220°C). Place a chicken breast smooth side down on a cutting board. Cover with two sheets of plastic wrap. With a meat hammer, gently pound the breast all over to widen and flatten it to about 1/4 inch (5 mm) thick. Repeat with the other chicken breasts. Combine the raisins, pine nuts, egg, spinach, salt and pepper in a bowl and mix well. Place an equal amount of the filling in the centre of each breast. Fold two sides of the breast partially over the filling, and then tightly roll it up to seal the filling inside. Place the breasts on a non-stick or parchment-lined baking tray. Brush the chicken with a little olive oil and season with salt and pepper. Bake for 20–25 minutes, or until cooked through.

While the chicken cooks, place the tomato sauce, sugar, lemon juice, orange juice, salt and pepper in a pot. Cover and gently simmer on medium-low heat for 10–15 minutes. Stir in the mint or basil and set aside on low heat until the chicken is cooked. Serve the chicken on a pool of sauce. For a more elegant presentation, slice the chicken into rounds, and fan the rounds over the sauce.

GRILLED CHICKEN with SUMMER BERRIES and GOAT CHEESE

preparation time ·	15 minutes
cooking time ·	6–8 minutes
makes ·	2 servings

This cool, vibrant combination is ideal for lunch or dinner on a hot summer day.

ERIC'S OPTIONS
If you want to spend more time with your guest, grill the chicken in advance, cool, and refrigerate until needed. If fresh berries are unavailable, substitute thinly sliced apples, peaches or pears.

2	6-oz. (175-g) boneless, skinless chicken breasts	2
1 Tbsp.	olive oil	15 mL
to taste	salt and black pepper	to taste
1/2 tsp.	Dijon mustard	2 mL
1 tsp.	honey	5 mL
1 Tbsp.	raspberry or balsamic vinegar	15 mL
2 Tbsp.	olive oil	25 mL
2 tsp.	chopped fresh tarragon, or 1/2 tsp. (2 mL) dried	10 mL
to taste	salt and black pepper	to taste
3 cups	organic baby salad greens	750 mL
4 oz.	soft goat cheese	125 g
1 cup	fresh berries, such as raspberries, blueberries and blackberries	250 mL
1/4 cup	pecan halves	50 mL

Brush the chicken with the 1 Tbsp. (15 mL) olive oil and season with salt and pepper. Grill over medium-high heat for 3–4 minutes per side, or until cooked through. Cool to room temperature.

Place the Dijon mustard, honey, vinegar, remaining 2 Tbsp. (25 mL) olive oil, tarragon, salt and pepper in a large bowl. Whisk to combine. Add the salad greens to the dressing and toss to coat the greens well. Divide the greens between 2 dinner plates. Slice the chicken at a slight angle and fan it over the greens. Set small pieces of the goat cheese, berries and pecans around the chicken. Serve immediately.

HONEY and CITRUS–GLAZED CHICKEN BREAST

preparation time · 10 minutes
cooking time · 20–25 minutes
makes · 4 servings

Serve this easy to make chicken with Roasted Pepper and Spinach Salad (page 24).

ERIC'S OPTIONS
The chicken is equally delicious served cold and is a good item to take on a picnic. Cool to room temperature after cooking, chill for several hours in the fridge, and slice before safely packing it away in a cooler for the trip to the picnic site.

4	6-oz. (175-g) boneless, skinless chicken breasts	4
1/4 cup	honey	50 mL
2 Tbsp.	lemon juice	25 mL
2 Tbsp.	orange juice	25 mL
2 tsp.	Dijon mustard	10 mL
to taste	salt and freshly cracked black pepper	to taste

Preheat the oven to 400°F (200°C). Place the chicken in a small, lightly oiled or non-stick baking dish. Combine the remaining ingredients in a bowl and then pour over the chicken. Bake, basting occasionally, for 20–25 minutes, or until cooked through. Broil the chicken for 1–2 minutes to glaze the top.

CORNMEAL-CRUSTED CHICKEN LEGS

preparation time · 15 minutes
cooking time · 45–50 minutes
makes · 4 servings

Cornmeal and honey give this chicken an irresistibly crisp crust. It can be served hot or cold. When kept safely chilled, it is ideal summer picnic fare.

ERIC'S OPTIONS
For an even crunchier crust, replace the bread crumbs with finely crushed corn flakes. For a calorie-reduced version of this dish, remove the skin from the chicken before coating.

3/4 cup	cornmeal	175 mL
3/4 cup	bread crumbs	175 mL
pinch	cayenne pepper	pinch
to taste	salt and freshly cracked black pepper	to taste
4	large chicken legs, cut into leg and thigh pieces	4
1/3 cup	Dijon mustard	75 mL
2–3 Tbsp.	liquid honey, warmed slightly	25–45 mL

Preheat the oven to 400°F (200°C). Combine the cornmeal, bread crumbs, cayenne, salt and pepper in a shallow-sided dish. Brush the chicken all over with the mustard. Place the chicken in the crust mixture and pat the mixture onto the chicken to coat it on all sides. Set on a baking sheet skin side down and bake for 20 minutes. Turn the pieces over and bake for 15 minutes more. Drizzle the top of the chicken with honey and bake for 10–15 minutes more, or until cooked through.

GARLIC-STUFFED CHICKEN LEGS
with PAN GRAVY

preparation time · 20 minutes
cooking time · 50–60 minutes
makes · 4 servings

Serve this with a couple of favourite vegetables and Buttermilk Yukon Gold Mashed Potatoes (page 151) and you'll have a very comforting, budget-friendly supper.

ERIC'S OPTIONS
Use bone-in chicken breasts instead of legs. Carefully stuff the garlic under the skin and proceed as directed in the recipe. Cooking time may be a little less, depending on the size of the breasts.

4	large chicken legs	4
6	garlic cloves, thinly sliced	6
1 tsp.	dried herbs, such as sage, thyme and rosemary	5 mL
to taste	salt and freshly cracked black pepper	to taste
2 1/2 cups	chicken stock	625 mL
3 Tbsp.	all-purpose flour	45 mL
to taste	salt and freshly cracked black pepper	to taste

Preheat the oven to 400°F (200°C). Carefully lift the skin from the thigh end of a chicken leg. Stuff 1/4 of the garlic slices underneath, pushing them to different points around the leg. Repeat with the remaining legs. Place the chicken in a stovetop and ovenproof pan. Sprinkle the herbs over the chicken and season with salt and pepper. Bake, basting with the pan juices occasionally, for 45–50 minutes, or until cooked through.

When the chicken is ready, remove it from the pan and keep it warm. Remove excess fat from the pan and set over medium heat. Pour in 2 cups (500 mL) of the stock. Mix the flour with the remaining 1/2 cup (125 mL) of stock until it is lump-free. Add it to the pan in a slow stream, whisking constantly. Bring the gravy to a simmer and cook until it thickens and the flour is cooked through. Season with salt and pepper. Serve the chicken with the gravy alongside.

TERIYAKI CHICKEN and VEGETABLE STIR-FRY

preparation time	·	15 minutes
cooking time	·	15 minutes
makes	·	4 servings

This dish is easy, quick and colourful, and it's all made in one pan. All you need to complete the meal is a pot of steamed rice.

ERIC'S OPTIONS
Try using thin-cut pork chops or small tender beef steaks, about 1 inch (2.5 cm) thick, instead of chicken. Cook as for the chicken, reducing the time a little if you like your beef rare.

2 Tbsp.	vegetable oil	25 mL
4	6-oz. (175-g) boneless skinless chicken breasts	4
to taste	salt and freshly cracked black pepper	to taste
1/4 cup	cornstarch	50 mL
1	medium red bell pepper, halved, seeded and sliced	1
1	medium carrot, thinly sliced	1
1 cup	pineapple chunks, tinned or fresh	250 mL
4	green onions, cut into 1-inch (2.5-cm) pieces	4
1/2–3/4 cup	teriyaki sauce	125–175 mL

Heat the oil in large skillet over medium-high heat. Season the chicken with salt and pepper and then lightly coat in cornstarch, shaking the excess off. Cook the chicken for 2–3 minutes on each side. Remove from the pan and set aside. Add the bell pepper and carrot to the pan and stir-fry for 2–3 minutes. Stir in the pineapple and green onions. Set the chicken on top of mixture and pour the teriyaki sauce into the pan. Cover, reduce the heat to medium, and cook until the vegetables are tender and the chicken is cooked through, about 3–5 minutes.

HOW TO STIR-FRY

Stir-frying is a cooking technique where small pieces of food are quickly cooked over high heat. Meats and seafood sear on the outside, keeping them moist and tender in the middle. Vegetables retain a brilliant colour and a crisp-tender texture. A wok or large skillet is the best tool to use as it offers a wide, hot surface for the foods to be moved around and rapidly cooked. Because of the quick cooking time it's important to have all ingredients chopped and ready to go. Heat the pan and cooking oil before you add the ingredients. If you don't, vegetables meant to be crisp can turn limp and meats may stick to the bottom of the pan. Use peanut or good-quality vegetable oil for stir-frying; they have a neutral flavour and can be heated to high temperatures without burning.

ONE-PAN MEDITERRANEAN-STYLE CHICKEN DINNER

preparation time · 20 minutes
cooking time · 45–50 minutes
makes · 4 servings

Here's a one-pan way to make a delicious chicken dinner — and to make it even easier, you can prepare the vegetables early in the day and refrigerate them.

ERIC'S OPTIONS
If you don't have fresh herbs, substitute 2 tsp. (10 mL) dried. Toss them in with the vegetables before they're placed in the casserole.

2	medium onions, cut into wedges	2
4	garlic cloves, sliced	4
1	large red bell pepper, seeded and cubed	1
1	14-oz. (398-mL) can artichoke hearts, drained well and quartered	1
12–16	small new potatoes, halved and parboiled until just tender	12–16
2 Tbsp.	olive oil	25 mL
to taste	salt and black pepper	to taste
1 cup	chicken stock	250 mL
4	bone-in chicken breasts or legs	4
1	large lemon, cut into 8 thin rounds	1
2 Tbsp.	chopped fresh oregano, basil or parsley	25 mL

Preheat the oven to 375°F (190°C). Place the onions, garlic, bell pepper, artichokes and potatoes in a bowl. Toss with 1 Tbsp. (15 mL) of the olive oil and the salt and pepper. Place the vegetables in a casserole. Add the chicken stock. Place the chicken on top of the vegetables, brush it with the remaining 1 Tbsp. (15 mL) of olive oil, and season with salt and pepper. Top the chicken with lemon slices. Roast for 45–50 minutes, or until the chicken is golden brown and cooked through. Baste the chicken and vegetables with the pan juices a few times during cooking. Sprinkle on the fresh herbs near the end of cooking. Arrange the chicken and vegetables on dinner plates, spoon the pan juices over top and serve.

QUICK and EASY CHICKEN ENCHILADAS

preparation time	·	20–25 minutes
cooking time	·	20–25 minutes
makes	·	4 servings

To round out this meal, serve the enchiladas with steamed or Spanish-style rice, refried beans, shredded lettuce, sliced avocados and, if desired, a dollop of light or regular sour cream.

ERIC'S OPTIONS			
Sliced turkey breast, pork loin or tender beef could replace the chicken.	2 Tbsp.	olive oil	25 mL
	1 1/2 lbs.	boneless, skinless chicken breasts or thighs, sliced into thin strips	750 g
	to taste	salt and freshly cracked black pepper	to taste
	3 cups	tomato sauce	750 ml
	1 tsp.	ground cumin	5 mL
	2 tsp.	chili powder	10 mL
	1/4 tsp.	cayenne pepper, or to taste	1 mL
	2 cups	grated Cheddar or Monterey Jack cheese	500 mL
	4	10-inch (25-cm) tortillas	4

Preheat the oven to 375°F (190°C). Heat the oil in a skillet over medium-high heat. Season the chicken with salt and pepper, place in the skillet, and cook through, about 5–6 minutes. Remove from the heat and set aside.

Combine the tomato sauce, cumin, chili powder and cayenne in a bowl. Combine half this mixture with the chicken. Add half the cheese and mix well. Divide the mixture between the tortillas, placing it along the centre of each. Roll each tortilla into a cylinder. Place seam side down on a parchment-lined or non-stick baking tray, spacing them about 2 inches (5 cm) apart. Top with the remaining sauce and cheese. Bake for 20–25 minutes.

SAGE and MUSTARD-CRUSTED CORNISH GAME HEN

preparation time · 15 minutes
cooking time · 45–50 minutes
makes · 2 servings

A large Cornish hen makes an ideal dinner for two.

ERIC'S OPTIONS
This style of crust also works well with regular chicken halves or pieces. Adjust the cooking time and ingredient amounts as required. An equal amount of fresh or dried rosemary could be used instead of the sage.

1	1 1/2-lb. (750-g) Cornish game hen	1
2 Tbsp.	Dijon mustard	25 mL
1/4 cup	bread crumbs	50 mL
2 Tbsp.	freshly grated Parmesan cheese	25 mL
to taste	salt and freshly cracked black pepper	to taste
1 Tbsp.	finely chopped fresh sage, or 1 tsp. (5 mL) dried	15 mL

Preheat the oven to 425°F (220°C). With kitchen shears or a knife, cut along either side of the hen's backbone and remove. Press the hen flat, skin side down, and then cut it in half down the middle of the breast bone. Turn the pieces over and brush the skin side with mustard. Place the remaining ingredients in a shallow-sided plate. Coat the mustard side of the pieces with the bread crumb mixture, gently patting it on. Place the pieces crust side up in a baking dish. Roast for 45–50 minutes, or until cooked through.

CORNISH GAME HENS with ORANGE, ROSEMARY and CRANBERRY GLAZE

preparation time · 25 minutes
cooking time · 45 – 50 minutes
makes · 6 servings

Consider this festive dish when planning a special dinner. It makes a fine substitute for turkey at Thanksgiving or Christmas.

ERIC'S OPTIONS
Use an equal amount of orange marmalade or black currant jam or jelly instead of the cranberry sauce in the glaze. Add a touch more vinegar if the ingredient you add is sweeter than the cranberry sauce.

3	1 1/2-lb. (750-g) Cornish game hens	3
1 Tbsp.	olive oil	15 mL
to taste	salt and freshly cracked black pepper	to taste
3/4 cup	jellied cranberry sauce	175 mL
2 tsp.	orange zest	10 mL
1/4 cup	orange juice	50 mL
1 Tbsp.	chopped fresh rosemary	15 mL
1 Tbsp.	brown sugar	15 mL
1 Tbsp.	red wine vinegar	15 mL
	fresh rosemary sprigs	

Preheat the oven to 425°F (220°C). With kitchen shears or a knife, cut along either side of each hen's backbone and remove. Press the hens flat, skin side down, and then cut each in half down the middle of the breast bone. Place the pieces skin side up on a baking sheet or large roasting pan. Brush lightly with olive oil and season with salt and pepper. Roast the hens for 20 minutes while you make the glaze.

Place the cranberry sauce, orange zest and juice, chopped rosemary, sugar and vinegar in a pot. Cook, stirring, over medium heat until the cranberry sauce melts and the sauce lightly thickens. After the hens have roasted for 20 minutes, brush them with half the glaze. Roast for 10 minutes more, and then brush with most of the remaining glaze, reserving a little to give the hens a shine just before serving. Roast the hens until cooked, about 15–20 minutes more. Arrange on plates or a platter, brush with the last of the glaze and garnish with fresh rosemary sprigs.

TURKEY SHEPHERD'S PIE with YUKON GOLD MASHED POTATOES

preparation time · 30 minutes
cooking time · 30–40 minutes
makes · 6 servings

This twist on the classic casserole can be readied ahead, cooled, refrigerated, and then cooked later that day or the next. It also freezes very well unbaked.

ERIC'S OPTIONS
Use other ground meats, such as beef or lamb, instead of turkey. For tangy potatoes, replace the milk with buttermilk.

2½–3 lbs.	Yukon Gold potatoes, peeled and quartered	1.25–1.5 kg
2 Tbsp.	olive or vegetable oil	25 mL
1½ lbs.	ground turkey	750 g
1	medium onion, finely chopped	1
1	small carrot, grated	1
2	garlic cloves, chopped	2
1 tsp.	dried thyme	5 mL
2 Tbsp.	all-purpose flour	25 mL
1 cup	tomato sauce	250 mL
1 cup	chicken stock	250 mL
1 cup	frozen (thawed) peas	250 mL
1 cup	frozen (thawed) corn	250 mL
to taste	salt, black pepper and Worcestershire sauce	to taste
2 Tbsp.	butter	25 mL
½–¾ cup	milk	125–175 mL
3–4	green onions, finely chopped	3–4
to taste	salt and freshly cracked black pepper	to taste

Preheat the oven to 375°F (190°C). Boil the potatoes until very tender. While the potatoes are cooking, heat the oil in a large skillet over medium-high heat. Add the ground turkey, onion, carrot, garlic and thyme. Cook, stirring to break the turkey into small pieces, until the meat is cooked through. Stir in the flour, and then mix in the tomato sauce, stock, peas and corn. Season with salt, pepper and Worcestershire sauce. Bring just to a simmer, remove from the heat, and spoon into a 9 x 13-inch (23 x 33-cm) baking dish.

Mash the potatoes, and then whip in the butter, milk and green onions. Season the potatoes with salt and pepper. Spread or pipe the potatoes over the turkey mixture. (If you are making the shepherd's pie in advance, cool to room temperature, wrap and then refrigerate or freeze. If freezing, thaw in the refrigerator overnight before baking.) Bake the shepherd's pie for 30–40 minutes (a little longer if it has been refrigerated), until the potatoes are golden and the filling is bubbling.

HEAVENLY SPICED TURKEY and VEGETABLE KEBABS

preparation time ·	30–40 minutes	
cooking time ·	8–10 minutes	
makes ·	4 servings	

Cumin, coriander, ginger and turmeric give the turkey an inviting aroma, a rich golden colour, and a heavenly Middle Eastern–style taste. These kebabs are a good match for Romaine with Oranges, Feta and Olives (page 19). If you are using wooden skewers, soak them in cold water for several hours before making the kebabs.

THE MARINADE	2	garlic cloves, crushed	2
	2 tsp.	freshly grated ginger	10 mL
	1/2	lemon, juiced	1/2
	3 Tbsp.	olive oil	45 mL
	1/4 tsp.	ground turmeric	1 mL
	1/2 tsp.	ground coriander	2 mL
	1/2 tsp.	ground cumin	2 mL
	pinch	cayenne pepper	pinch
	1 tsp.	freshly cracked black pepper	5 mL
	1/4 cup	grated onion	50 mL

THE KEBABS	1 1/4–1 1/2 lbs.	boneless, skinless turkey breast, cut into 16 cubes	625–750 g
	1	large white onion, cut into 16 wedges	1
	1	large green bell pepper, cut into 16 chunks	1
	1	large red bell pepper, cut into 16 chunks	1
	to taste	salt	to taste

THE MARINADE
Mix all the marinade ingredients in a large bowl.

THE KEBABS
Place the turkey in the marinade, toss to evenly coat and then refrigerate for 4 hours. Preheat the barbecue or indoor grill to medium. Thread the turkey and vegetables onto 4 long skewers, alternating the meat and vegetables for an attractive presentation. Lightly oil the grill. Grill the kebabs, turning to cook them on all sides, for approximately 8–10 minutes, or until the meat is cooked through.

ERIC'S OPTIONS
Use tender boneless chicken, pork, beef or lamb instead of the turkey.

SPICE-ROASTED DUCK
with HOISIN GLAZE

preparation time	·	30 minutes
cooking time	·	1 3/4 – 2 hours
makes	·	3 – 4 servings

The wonderful aromas of five-spice, ginger and hoisin sauce will fill your house as the duck roasts. Close your windows if you don't want your neighbours knocking on the door looking for an invitation to dinner!

NOTE

This style of duck is often served with thin pancakes that are used to wrap up delicious morsels of meat and a little hoisin sauce. However, for a quicker and lighter alternative, I like to use small whole lettuce leaves, such as butter, leaf or iceberg, to wrap the meat. Steamed rice and a mound of quickly stir-fried vegetables would also go great with the duck.

1	4- to 5-lb. (2- to 2.2-kg) duck, rinsed in cold water and patted dry	1
5 Tbsp.	soy sauce	75 mL
1/2 cup	white wine or dry sherry	125 mL
1/2 tsp.	salt	2 mL
3 tsp.	five-spice powder	15 mL
1 Tbsp.	vegetable oil	15 mL
1	medium onion, halved and sliced	1
2 Tbsp.	coarsely chopped ginger	25 mL
3	garlic cloves, crushed	3
2 Tbsp.	hoisin sauce, plus some to serve with the cooked duck	25 mL

Using a fork, prick the skin of the duck all over. Combine 2 Tbsp. (25 mL) of the soy sauce, white wine or sherry, salt and 2 tsp. (10 mL) of the five-spice powder in a large bowl. Add the duck and brush it with the mixture inside and out. Cover and marinate in the refrigerator for 4 hours, turning and basting the duck from time to time.

Heat the oil in a pot over medium-high heat. Add the onion, ginger and garlic and cook for 2–3 minutes. Add 2 Tbsp. (25 mL) of the soy sauce and the remaining

1 tsp. (5 mL) of five-spice powder. Cook for 2 minutes more. Remove from heat and cool. Stuff this mixture inside the duck and use skewers or string to enclose it. Tie the legs together with string and fold the wings under the body.

Preheat the oven to 425°F (220°C). Place the duck, breast side up, on a rack in a roasting pan. Fill the pan with hot water to a level just below the duck. Cover tightly so the water in the pan will steam the duck. Roast for 90 minutes.

Increase the heat to 475°F (240°C). Make the hoisin glaze by combining the hoisin sauce with the remaining 1 Tbsp. (15 mL) of soy sauce in a small bowl. Uncover the duck and brush with the glaze. Roast, uncovered, until the skin is richly glazed and crispy, about 20–30 minutes.

Allow the duck to rest for 10–15 minutes before carving. Thinly slice the meat, arrange it on a platter, and serve it with extra hoisin sauce alongside.

ERIC'S OPTIONS
The stuffing in this dish infuses incredible flavour into the meat but is not meant to be eaten. However, the duck carcass with stuffing makes a delicious soup stock. Simmer, just covered in water, for 1 1/2–2 hours. For a quick soup, simmer any left-over duck meat and Chinese-style vegetables, such as bok choy and Chinese cabbage, in the stock for a few minutes, then pour it over some cooked Chinese-style noodles. Sprinkle with green onions and serve. Flavour the soup with a little soy sauce and hot sauce if desired.

Halibut and Spinach
Wrapped in Filo, 64

Cornmeal-
Crusted
Crab Cakes
with Cayenne
Mayonnaise, 74

Cornmeal-
Crusted
Chicken
Legs, 98

Cornish Game Hens with Orange, Rosemary and Cranberry Glaze, 105

Spice-Roasted
Duck with Hoisin
Glaze, 110

Prosciutto-Wrapped Pork
Loin with Salsa Verde, 133

Lamb Shanks Braised with
Tomatoes, Rosemary and Garlic, 128

Pork Side Ribs
with Chipotle
Barbecue
Sauce, 134

Veal-Stuffed
Pasta Shells
with Olive
Tomato
Sauce, 54

Tortellini
Soup with
Italian Sausage
and Crumbled
Feta, 39

Grilled Sirloin on Rice Noodles with
Green Onions, Garlic and Ginger, 58

Southern-Style Short Ribs	114
Grandma Akis's Hamburger Steaks	116
Cheryl's Beef and Potato Moussaka	118
Glazed Meatloaf with Onion Gravy	120
Chunky Chili with Dark Ale	122
Pot Roast Braised with Port and Rosemary	124
Eric's Tourtière	126
Lamb Shanks Braised with Tomatoes, Rosemary and Garlic	128

MEATY
MAINS

CHAPTER EIGHT

Lamb Chops with Blackcurrant Sauce	130
Lemony Lamb Chops with Artichokes, Olives and Mint	132
Prosciutto-Wrapped Pork Loin with Salsa Verde	133
Pork Side Ribs with Chipotle Barbecue Sauce	134
Oak Bay Baked Beans	136
Pan-Seared Pork Cutlets with Grainy Mustard Sauce	138

SOUTHERN-STYLE SHORT RIBS

preparation time	·	30 minutes
cooking time	·	2–2½ hours
makes	·	4 servings

Roasting short ribs in a hot oven prior to braising helps render away much of the excess fat. Serve these ribs with Blue Cheese Biscuits (page 141) to soak up the delectable sauce.

ERIC'S OPTIONS
Use 8–12 beef back ribs (prime rib or standing rib bones) in place of the short ribs. For a smoky chili taste, add 2–3 finely chopped chipotle peppers to the tomato mixture before spooning it over the short ribs.

2 tsp.	ground cumin	10 mL
2 tsp.	chili powder	10 mL
1 tsp.	ground coriander	5 mL
1 tsp.	dried thyme	5 mL
1 tsp.	dried oregano	5 mL
1 tsp.	salt	5 mL
1 tsp.	freshly cracked black pepper	5 mL
¼ tsp.	cayenne pepper	1 mL
8–12	2-inch-thick (5-cm) beef short ribs	8–12
1	medium onion, coarsely chopped	1
2	garlic cloves, halved and sliced	2
1½ cups	tomato sauce	375 mL
1 cup	beef stock	250 mL
1 Tbsp.	brown sugar	15 mL
2 Tbsp.	chopped cilantro or fresh parsley	25 mL

Preheat the oven to 450°F (230°C). In a small bowl combine the cumin, chili powder, coriander, thyme, oregano, salt, pepper and cayenne. Rub the spice mix on the ribs. Place the ribs in a roasting pan just large enough to hold them and roast for 30 minutes. Remove from the oven and drain away the excess fat. Reduce the oven temperature to 325°F (160°C).

Combine the onion, garlic, tomato sauce, stock and brown sugar in a bowl. Pour over the ribs. Cover and bake for 1 1/2–2 hours, or until the meat is very tender and falling off the bone. Transfer the ribs to a serving platter. Skim the fat from the sauce and adjust the seasoning. Spoon the sauce over the ribs, sprinkle with cilantro or parsley and serve.

GRANDMA AKIS'S HAMBURGER STEAKS

preparation time	·	20–25 minutes
cooking time	·	10–12 minutes
makes	·	4 servings

These hamburger steaks were a staple item in my Latvian grandmother's culinary repertoire. The milk in her hamburger mixture added richness and made the steaks more tender. The mushroom sauce is something I added later. This dish goes well with buttered peas and carrots and boiled, steamed or mashed potatoes.

THE HAMBURGER STEAKS	1 1/4 lbs.	lean ground beef	625 g
	1	large egg, beaten	1
	3	green onions, finely chopped	3
	2	garlic cloves, crushed	2
	1/2 cup	bread crumbs	125 mL
	1/4 cup	milk	50 mL
	2 Tbsp.	Worcestershire sauce	25 mL
	1/2 tsp.	dried thyme	2 mL
	1 tsp.	salt	5 mL
	1 tsp.	freshly ground black pepper	5 mL
	2 Tbsp.	vegetable oil	25 mL
THE MUSHROOM SAUCE	3 Tbsp.	vegetable oil	45 mL
	1/2	medium onion, finely chopped	1/2
	1/2 lb.	white or brown mushrooms, thinly sliced	250 g
	3 Tbsp.	all-purpose flour	45 mL
	2 cups	beef stock	500 mL
	to taste	salt and freshly cracked black pepper	to taste

THE HAMBURGER STEAKS

Place all the ingredients, except for the oil, in a bowl and gently mix to combine. (Do not overmix or you will compact the meat and the resulting steaks will have a firm, tough texture when cooked.) Moisten your hands with water and form the meat mixture into 4 oval patties, 3/4 inch (2 cm) thick. Heat the oil in a non-stick skillet over medium to medium-high heat. Cook the hamburger steaks for 4–5 minutes per side, or until entirely cooked through.

THE MUSHROOM SAUCE

Heat the oil in a pot over medium-high heat. Add the onion and mushrooms and cook until tender. Mix in the flour until well combined. Slowly mix in the stock. Bring to a simmer and cook until the gravy thickens. Season with salt and pepper. Serve the gravy on or alongside the hamburger steaks.

ERIC'S OPTIONS
For a more complex flavour use a mixture of ground beef, pork and veal. Use half a medium onion, finely chopped, instead of the green onions.

CHERYL'S BEEF and POTATO MOUSSAKA

preparation time	·	40 minutes
cooking time	·	60–70 minutes
makes	·	6–8 servings

This is my wife's delicious rendition of the classic Greek dish. She serves it with Greek salad and grilled pita bread.

ERIC'S OPTIONS
You can make this with ground lamb instead of beef or use thin slices of eggplant instead of potatoes.

1 1/2 lbs.	lean ground beef	750 g
1	large onion, finely chopped	1
2	garlic cloves, crushed	2
1	5 1/2-oz. (156-mL) can tomato paste	1
3/4 cup	water	175 mL
1/4 cup	chopped fresh parsley	50 mL
1 tsp.	dried mint	5 mL
1 tsp.	ground cinnamon	5 mL
to taste	salt and freshly cracked black pepper	to taste
8	medium potatoes	8
1/4 cup	butter	50 mL
1/4 cup	all-purpose flour	50 mL
2 cups	milk	500 mL
4	large eggs	4
1/2 cup	grated Parmesan cheese	125 mL
to taste	salt and freshly cracked black pepper	to taste

Preheat the oven to 375°F (190°C). Place the meat, onion and garlic in a pot and cook over medium heat, stirring frequently, until the meat is no longer pink. Drain off the fat. Add the tomato paste, water, parsley, mint, cinnamon, salt and pepper. Simmer until thickened, about 10 minutes. Remove from the heat and set aside. Peel the potatoes and slice them thinly. Place the slices in cold water as you work.

For the moussaka sauce, melt the butter in a pot over medium heat. Add the flour and stir and cook until it's absorbed by the butter. Slowly whisk in the milk. Simmer, stirring, just until the sauce thickens. Remove from the heat. Beat the eggs to a slight froth in a bowl. Mix 1/2 cup (125 mL) of the white sauce into the eggs, whisking constantly until well combined. Whisk this mixture back into the white sauce in the pot. Mix 6 Tbsp. (90 mL) of the Parmesan cheese into the mixture. Season to taste with salt and pepper.

To assemble the moussaka, lightly butter a 9 x 13-inch (23 x 33-cm) baking dish. Drain the potatoes well and arrange half the slices in the bottom of the dish. Pour half the moussaka sauce over the potatoes. Top with the meat mixture. Place the remaining potatoes over the meat and top with the remaining moussaka sauce. Sprinkle with the remaining 2 Tbsp. (25 mL) Parmesan cheese. Bake for 60–70 minutes, or until the potatoes are tender and the top is browned. Test for doneness by inserting the point of a small knife in the centre of the moussaka to see if the potatoes are cooked. Let the moussaka rest for 10 minutes to allow it to set before cutting into serving portions.

GLAZED MEATLOAF
with ONION GRAVY

preparation time · 20 minutes
cooking time · 1–1¼ hours
makes · 4–6 servings

You can never have too many recipes for meatloaf. Here's my version; you can make it in a loaf pan or on a baking sheet.

THE GLAZE	1/2 cup	sweet chili sauce or ketchup	125 mL
	2 Tbsp.	brown sugar	25 mL
	1 Tbsp.	red wine or cider vinegar	15 mL
THE MEATLOAF	3/4 lb.	lean ground beef	375 g
	3/4 lb.	ground pork	375 g
	2	large eggs, beaten	2
	4	green onions, finely chopped	4
	2	garlic cloves, chopped	2
	1/2 cup	bread crumbs	125 mL
	1/4 cup	milk	50 mL
	1/2 cup	sweet chili sauce or ketchup	125 mL
	1 tsp.	dried thyme	5 mL
	1 tsp.	salt	5 mL
	1 tsp.	freshly cracked black pepper	5 mL
THE GRAVY	3 Tbsp.	butter or vegetable oil	45 mL
	1	medium onion, finely chopped	1
	1/4 cup	flour	50 mL
	2 1/2 cups	hot beef stock	625 mL
	to taste	salt and freshly cracked black pepper	to taste

THE GLAZE
Combine all the ingredients in a small bowl.

THE MEATLOAF
Preheat the oven to 350°F (180°C). Place all the meatloaf ingredients in a bowl and gently mix to combine. Place the mixture in a non-stick or lightly oiled 9 x 5-inch (23 x 12.5-cm) loaf pan. (You could also shape it into a free-form loaf of similar size on a non-stick or parchment-lined baking sheet.) Spread the glaze ingredients over the meatloaf. Bake for 1–1¼ hours, or until cooked through. A meat thermometer inserted in the centre of the meatloaf should read 170°F (75°C).

THE GRAVY
When the meatloaf is almost done, you can make the gravy. Heat the butter or oil in a pot over medium to medium-high heat. Add the onion and cook until tender. Mix in the flour and cook until the mixture turns a very light brown. Slowly whisk in the beef stock. Simmer until thickened. Season with salt and pepper. Keep warm over low heat.

When the meatloaf is done, remove from the oven, cover and let it rest for 10 minutes. Drain any fat from the pan before unmoulding the meatloaf. Slice and serve with the gravy alongside.

ERIC'S OPTIONS
Ground turkey could replace the beef and pork. Use barbecue sauce instead of sweet chili sauce or ketchup. Use ½ medium onion, finely chopped, instead of the green onions.

CHUNKY CHILI
with DARK ALE

preparation time	·	30 minutes
cooking time	·	1 1/2–2 hours
makes	·	8 servings

I like to serve this stick-to-your-ribs chili when I have a gang over to watch the game. It goes well with Monterey Jack and Jalapeño Cornbread (page 140). It is also nice spooned over baked potatoes, baked sweet potatoes or steamed rice.

ERIC'S OPTIONS
For added richness top each bowl of chili with some grated Cheddar or Monterey Jack cheese, or add a dollop of sour cream or thick yogurt. Canned black-eyed peas, black beans, pinto beans, or a mix of beans could replace the kidney beans. Chili can be made up to 2 days in advance, refrigerated and reheated.

2 Tbsp.	vegetable oil	25 mL
3/4 lb.	blade or chuck steak, cut into 1/2-inch (1-cm) cubes	375 g
3/4 lb.	lean ground pork	375 g
1	medium onion, halved and cut into 1/2-inch (1-cm) cubes	1
1	medium green pepper, seeded and cut into 1/2-inch (1-cm) cubes	1
1	medium red pepper, seeded and cut into 1/2-inch (1-cm) cubes	1
1	medium yellow pepper, seeded and cut into 1/2-inch (1-cm) cubes	1
2	garlic cloves, chopped	2
1	14-oz. (398-mL) can crushed tomatoes	1
1	14-oz. (398-mL) can diced tomatoes	1
1	19-oz. (532-mL) can red or white kidney beans, rinsed and drained well	1
1 Tbsp.	hot pepper sauce (or to taste)	15 mL
12 oz.	dark ale	340 mL
3/4 cup	beef stock	175 mL
3 Tbsp.	chili powder	45 mL

2 tsp.	ground cumin	10 mL
2 tsp.	dry mustard	10 mL
3 Tbsp.	brown sugar	45 mL
1 tsp.	dried oregano	5 mL
to taste	salt and freshly cracked black pepper	to taste

Heat the oil in a large, heavy pot or Dutch oven over medium-high heat. Add the beef, pork and onions and cook until the meat is no longer pink. Mix in the remaining ingredients. Cover, reduce the heat until the chili gently simmers, and cook for 1 1/2–2 hours, until the meat is tender and the chili is thick and bubbly. Stir occasionally. Thin with a little water if it becomes too thick.

POT ROAST BRAISED with PORT and ROSEMARY

preparation time	·	30–40 minutes
cooking time	·	2¼–2½ hours
makes	·	4–6 servings

Pot roast is not the most exciting dish around. But this one, thanks to flavour-enhancing ingredients such as port, Dijon mustard and shallots, is robust and rewarding. It is also relatively inexpensive to make and cooks in one pan.

ERIC'S OPTIONS
For a touch of spiciness, add 2–3 Tbsp. (25–45 mL) of green peppercorns to the pot when you add the port. You could replace the shallots with 2 medium onions, halved and sliced. If you don't have fresh rosemary, use 1 tsp. (5 mL) dried.

2 Tbsp.	vegetable oil	25 mL
2½–3 lbs.	chuck, blade or baron of beef roast, trimmed of excess fat	1.25–1.5 kg
to taste	salt and black pepper	to taste
2 cups	beef stock	500 mL
1 cup	port	250 mL
1 Tbsp.	chopped fresh rosemary	15 mL
2 Tbsp.	Dijon mustard	25 mL
1 Tbsp.	Worcestershire sauce	15 mL
1	bay leaf	1
3	cloves garlic, peeled and sliced	3
¼ cup	all-purpose flour	50 mL
½ cup	water	125 mL
1 lb.	baby carrots	500 g
12	small shallots, peeled	12
4	medium white potatoes, cut in quarters	4
	chopped green onion or fresh parsley	

Preheat the oven to 325°F (160°C). Heat the oil in a large Dutch oven or deep-sided roasting pan over medium-high heat. Season the roast with salt and pepper and brown it on all sides. Remove it from the pan and set aside. Drain the excess fat from the pan. Add the stock, port, rosemary, mustard, Worcestershire sauce, bay leaf and garlic to the pan and bring to a simmer. In a small bowl, blend the flour and water and slowly whisk it into the simmering mixture. Cook until the sauce thickens. Return the roast to the pot. Cover and cook in the oven for 1 3/4 hours, turning once.

Add the carrots, shallots and potatoes. If the sauce is too thick, add a little water. Cover and cook 30–45 minutes more, or until the vegetables and beef are tender.

Remove the meat from the pot, cover and let rest for 10 minutes. With a slotted spoon, scoop out the vegetables and arrange them on one side of a platter. Slice the beef and place it on the other side. Sprinkle with chopped green onions or fresh parsley. Ladle the sauce into a gravy boat and serve it alongside.

ERIC'S TOURTIÈRE

preparation time	·	40 minutes
cooking time	·	45–50 minutes
makes	·	6–8 servings

I serve my version of this classic French Canadian meat pie every Christmas Eve. Using a trio of ground meat gives it a more complex flavour. Make the filling the day before to allow the flavours to blend and develop. Serve the tourtière with pickled beets, mustard pickles, chutneys and relishes — homemade if you have them.

ERIC'S OPTIONS
Use either a store-bought or home-made pie crust (see Pastry for a Double Crust Pie, page 173). You can make the tourtière and freeze it unbaked. Thaw in the fridge overnight before baking.

1/2 lb.	ground veal	250 g
1/2 lb.	ground pork	250 g
1/2 lb.	ground beef	250 g
1	medium onion, diced	1
2	cloves garlic, chopped	2
1 tsp.	dried thyme	5 mL
1/2 tsp.	ground cloves	2 mL
1 1/2 tsp.	ground cinnamon	7.5 mL
2 Tbsp.	all-purpose flour	25 mL
1 1/4 cups	hot beef stock	300 mL
1 1/4 cups	water	300 mL
1 cup	small potato cubes, cooked firm-tender	250 mL
1 Tbsp.	chopped fresh parsley	15 mL
to taste	salt and black pepper	to taste
1	9-inch (23-cm) deep-dish double crust pie shell	1
	egg wash (1 large egg mixed with 2 Tbsp./25 mL milk)	

Place the meats, onion and garlic in a pot over medium heat. Cook until the meat is no longer pink, then drain away the fat. Add the thyme, cloves, cinnamon and flour and mix well. While stirring, slowly pour in the beef stock and water. Simmer until the liquid has almost evaporated, then mix in the potatoes and parsley. Season with salt and pepper. Remove from the heat, cool to room temperature and refrigerate overnight.

Preheat the oven to 425°F (220°C). Place the filling in the bottom pie crust. Brush the edges with egg wash. Place the top crust on, crimping the edges to seal. Decorate the top with extra pastry if desired. Brush the top of the pie with egg wash. Cut a small hole in the centre of the top crust to allow steam to escape. Bake for 20 minutes. Reduce the heat to 350°F (180°C) and cook 25–30 minutes more. Allow the tourtière to sit for about 10–15 minutes before slicing.

LAMB SHANKS BRAISED with TOMATOES, ROSEMARY and GARLIC

preparation time · 20 minutes
cooking time · 2–2¹/₂ hours
makes · 4 servings

Serve Balsamic Roasted Asparagus (page 146) and Orzo Baked with Green Onions and Parmesan (page 145) alongside these sumptuous lamb shanks. Lamb shanks can range in size, so choose portions to match the appetite of your guests.

ERIC'S OPTIONS
Veal shanks could replace the lamb. If you don't have fresh rosemary, use 1 tsp. (5 mL) dried.

1/2 cup	all-purpose flour	125 mL
2 Tbsp.	olive oil	25 mL
4	lamb shanks	4
to taste	salt and freshly cracked black pepper	to taste
1	medium onion, finely diced	1
4	garlic cloves, sliced	4
1 cup	red wine	250 mL
1	28-oz. (796-mL) can diced tomatoes	1
2 Tbsp.	tomato paste	25 mL
1 Tbsp.	chopped fresh rosemary	15 mL
2	bay leaves	2
1 Tbsp.	brown sugar	15 mL
1/2 tsp.	ground cinnamon	2 mL

Preheat the oven to 325°F (160°C). Place the flour on a plate. Heat the oil in a skillet over medium-high heat. While the oil is heating, season the lamb with salt and pepper and then dredge in the flour, shaking off the excess. Add the lamb to the skillet and brown on all sides. Place in a deep-sided casserole. Remove most of the fat from the pan. Add the onion and garlic and cook for 2 minutes. Add the remaining ingredients and bring to a simmer. Pour the mixture over the lamb shanks. Cover and cook for 2–2¹/₂ hours, or until the lamb is very tender. Adjust the seasoning and serve.

BRAISING AND STEWING MEAT

Braising and stewing are cooking methods designed to cook tougher cuts of meat to a succulent tenderness.

To braise meat, first brown it, then add a small amount of flavoured liquid, cover tightly and cook at a low temperature for a long period of time. (The meat should be surrounded by the liquid, not immersed in it.) Steam released from the liquid flavours and tenderizes the meat. It's important to have a tight lid, but additional liquid is sometimes required during the long cooking process. Braised meats are most often roasts or individual portions, such as lamb shanks.

For stewing, brown the meat and then entirely cover it in the stewing liquid. The meat is most often cut into bite-sized pieces and requires less cooking time.

Both braising and stewing can be done on the stovetop or in the oven. For both methods, I prefer to do the initial browning on the stovetop and finish the cooking in the oven. It cooks more evenly, won't stick or burn on the bottom, and allows me to do other things while the meat cooks.

LAMB CHOPS with
BLACKCURRANT SAUCE

preparation time · 5 minutes
cooking time · 10 minutes
makes · 2 servings

Sweet, sour and spicy flavours accent the lamb in this vibrant dish. To complete a spring feast, serve it with small new potatoes, baby carrots and asparagus.

ERIC'S OPTIONS
Use 1/2 tsp. (2 mL) dried mint instead of the fresh herb. Add it when you add the other sauce ingredients to the pan.

4–6	lamb chops	4–6
to taste	salt	to taste
1 Tbsp.	olive oil	15 mL
1 Tbsp.	finely chopped shallot or onion	15 mL
1 Tbsp.	balsamic vinegar	15 mL
1 tsp.	coarsely cracked black pepper	5 mL
1/4 cup	blackcurrant jelly or jam	50 mL
1/4 cup	red wine	50 mL
1 Tbsp.	chopped fresh mint	15 mL

Season the lamb with salt. Heat the oil in a small skillet over medium-high heat. Cook the lamb for 2–3 minutes per side, until it is nicely browned and partially cooked. Remove from the skillet and set aside. Place the shallot or onion in the skillet and cook for 1 minute. Add the vinegar, pepper, jelly or jam and wine, and simmer until the sauce thickens slightly. Sprinkle in the mint and return the lamb to the pan. Cook 3–4 minutes more, turning the chops. Adjust the seasonings and serve.

SUBSTITUTING DRIED HERBS FOR FRESH

The general rule of thumb when substituting dried herbs for fresh is to divide the amount called for by three. For example, if a recipe calls for 1 Tbsp. (15 mL) chopped fresh herb, you would use only use 1 tsp. (5 mL) dried. However, this can vary depending on the potency of the dried herb. For example, I find dried tarragon and dill to be very strong-tasting, so when substituting it for fresh I only use about half the amount noted above. Dried herbs need to be reconstituted and should be stirred into a dish before it starts cooking, not sprinkled on at the end of cooking as many fresh herbs are. When using dried herbs instead of fresh in a salad dressing or a dip, let it stand for an hour or so, refrigerated if necessary, to allow the dried herb to soften and release its flavour before mixing again and serving.

LEMONY LAMB CHOPS with ARTICHOKES, OLIVES and MINT

preparation time	·	20 minutes
cooking time	·	22 minutes
makes	·	4–6 servings

Serve this one-pan lamb dish with boiled new potatoes and Plum Tomato, Onion and Caper Salad (page 26).

ERIC'S OPTIONS
For another hit of flavour, add 1/4 cup (50 mL) of coarsely chopped sun-dried tomatoes to the casserole along with the artichokes and olives.

12	lamb chops, trimmed of excess fat	12
to taste	salt and freshly cracked black pepper	to taste
2–3 Tbsp.	olive oil	25–45 mL
1	14-oz. (398-mL) can quartered artichoke hearts	1
1/3 cup	whole black olives	75 mL
1/3 cup	whole green olives	75 mL
1	grated zest and juice of lemon	1
1 cup	white wine or chicken stock	250 mL
2 Tbsp.	chopped fresh mint	25 mL
	lemon slices	

Preheat the oven to 450°F (230°C). Season the lamb with salt and pepper. Heat the oil in a large skillet over medium-high heat and quickly brown the lamb on both sides. Transfer the chops to a casserole large enough to hold them in a single layer. Arrange the artichokes and olives around the lamb. Top with the lemon zest and juice. Pour in the wine or stock. Cover and bake for 20 minutes, or until the lamb reaches the desired degree of doneness. Uncover and sprinkle with the chopped mint. Garnish with lemon slices and serve.

PROSCIUTTO-WRAPPED PORK LOIN with SALSA VERDE

preparation time · 30 minutes
cooking time · 1¹/₄–1¹/₂ hours
makes · 6 servings

Salsa verde (green sauce) is an Italian-style sauce that can lift the flavour of any kind of meat or fish. In the summer, Roasted Pepper and Spinach Salad (page 24) makes a nice accompaniment. In the winter, serve it with steamed carrots tossed with butter and parsley and Orzo Baked with Green Onions and Parmesan (page 145).

ERIC'S OPTIONS
In summer I like to serve the pork cold. After roasting, cool the meat to room temperature, cover and refrigerate for several hours before slicing. Quick Rouille (page 143) is another sauce that goes well with the pork.

2¹/₂ lbs.	boneless pork loin	1.1 kg
to taste	freshly cracked black pepper	to taste
8	long, paper-thin slices prosciutto (see page 2)	8
¹/₄ cup	chopped fresh parsley	50 mL
¹/₄ cup	capers, finely chopped	50 mL
4	anchovy fillets, mashed	4
2	garlic cloves, finely chopped	2
1 tsp.	Dijon mustard	5 mL
1 tsp.	red wine vinegar	5 mL
¹/₂ cup	extra virgin olive oil	125 mL
to taste	salt and black pepper	to taste

Preheat the oven to 350°F (180°C). Season the pork with pepper (no need for salt as the prosciutto adds enough saltiness). Carefully wrap the slices of prosciutto, slightly over-lapping them, around the meat. Roast for 75–90 minutes, or until a meat thermometer inserted into the centre of the thickest part of the roast reaches 165°F (75°C).

While the pork is roasting, make the salsa verde. Combine the parsley, capers, anchovies, garlic, mustard and vinegar in a bowl. Slowly beat in the olive oil. Season with salt and pepper. Cover and set aside at room temperature. Leftover salsa verde can be stored in a sealed jar in the fridge for a week or so. Bring to room temperature before serving.

When the roast is cooked, let it rest for 10 minutes. Slice it thinly and serve the salsa verde alongside.

PORK SIDE RIBS with CHIPOTLE BARBECUE SAUCE

preparation time	·	20 minutes
cooking time	·	2 hours
makes	·	2–4 servings

Classic barbecue side dishes — potato salad, pickles, baked potatoes and corn on the cob — complement these ribs. Try the ribs with Southern-Spiced Coleslaw with Jicama and Corn (page 27).

ERIC'S OPTIONS
After the initial oven cooking, these ribs can be finished off on the barbecue. Preheat the grill to medium. Grill the ribs on both sides for a few minutes to accent their colour. Reduce the heat to low and brush the ribs on both sides with the sauce. Cook for 5–10 minutes more, or until nicely glazed.

2	whole racks pork side ribs	2
to taste	salt and freshly cracked black pepper	to taste
1 3/4 cups	beer	425 mL
2 Tbsp.	olive oil	25 mL
1	medium onion, finely chopped	1
2	garlic cloves, finely chopped	2
2–3	chipotle peppers, finely chopped	2–3
1 1/2 cups	ketchup	375 mL
2 tsp.	chili powder	10 mL
2 tsp.	dry mustard	10 mL
3 Tbsp.	brown sugar, packed	45 mL
2 Tbsp.	red wine vinegar	25 mL
2 tsp.	Worcestershire sauce	10 mL
to taste	salt	to taste

Preheat the oven to 325°F (160°C). Cut the racks in half. Lay them in a single layer in a baking dish. Season generously with salt and pepper and pour in 1 cup (250 mL) of the beer. Cover and bake for 90 minutes, or until the ribs are quite tender.

While the ribs are cooking, heat the oil in a pot over medium heat. Add the onion and garlic and cook until tender. Stir the remaining ingredients, including the ¾ cup (175 mL) beer, into the pot. Reduce the heat to medium-low, cover and very gently simmer for 30–40 minutes, stirring occasionally. Thin the sauce with a little water if it becomes too thick. Remove from the heat and set aside.

When the ribs are tender, carefully drain most of the liquid from the pan. Spoon the sauce over the ribs, reserving, if desired, 1 cup (250 mL) for a dip at the table. Bake the ribs uncovered for another 30 minutes, until they are nicely glazed.

NOTE
Chipotle peppers, which are smoked jalapeño peppers, are sold in cans and can be found in the Mexican food section of most supermarkets. The more you use, the spicier the ribs will be. Unused peppers can be placed in a tightly sealed jar and refrigerated for another use, such as chili or taco fillings.

OAK BAY
BAKED BEANS

preparation time · 1¹/₄–1¹/₂ hours (includes precooking the beans)
cooking time · 3–4 hours
makes · 8 servings as a main course, 12 as a side dish

For lack of a better name, I decided to call my version of baked beans after the area where I live. After placing my beans in the oven to bake one day, I went for my morning stroll. On the way back, at least a block from my house, I could smell their heavenly aroma wafting around the Oak Bay neighbourhood. I made my beans with pork, but this is an excellent vegetarian dish without the meat.

ERIC'S OPTIONS
The recipe can be halved. Try substituting lima beans or black-eyed peas for the small white beans. The time it takes to precook each legume will vary slightly.

2 lbs.	small white beans, presoaked if desired	1 kg
1/2 cup	maple syrup	125 mL
1/2 cup	molasses	125 mL
1/2 cup	barbecue sauce	125 mL
2	medium onions, chopped	2
2¹/₂ cups	tomato sauce	625 mL
2–3 tsp.	dry mustard	10–15 mL
1 Tbsp.	Worcestershire sauce	15 mL
2	bay leaves	2
1	smoked pork hock or 1/2 lb. (250 g) salt pork cut in 2 pieces (optional)	1
2 cups	cold water	500 mL
to taste	salt and freshly cracked black pepper	to taste

Place the beans in a large pot and cover with 3–4 inches (8–10 cm) of cold water. Bring to a boil, then reduce the heat to a gentle simmer. Cover and cook until tender, but still slightly firm to the bite. If you've presoaked the beans overnight in cold water, this will take about 45–60 minutes. If you cook unsoaked beans, it will take about 60–75 minutes. Skim away any foam that rises to the top as the beans cook. Add more water during cooking if required.

Preheat the oven to 300°F (150°C). Drain the beans and transfer to a Dutch oven or casserole with a capacity of 16–20 cups (4–5 L). In a bowl, combine the maple syrup, molasses, barbecue sauce, onions, tomato sauce, mustard and Worcestershire sauce. Stir into the beans. Nestle in the bay leaves and the pork hock or salt pork, if desired. Pour the 2 cups (500 mL) cold water over the beans. Cover and bake for 3–4 hours, or until the beans are tender. Check the beans occasionally during cooking and add more water if they become too dry.

If you included the pork, remove it when the beans are finished cooking, cut the edible portions into pieces and mix them back in. Season the beans with salt and pepper.

NOTE
The small white beans called for in this recipe are sometimes labelled white pea beans or navy beans. The older the beans, the longer they will take to cook. If they take forever to become tender, it's time to buy new ones. When purchasing beans, buy them from a location that sells a lot of them and therefore has a higher rate of turnover.

PAN-SEARED PORK CUTLETS
with GRAINY MUSTARD SAUCE

preparation time · 5 minutes
cooking time · 10–12 minutes
makes · 4 servings

Serve these quick and easy cutlets with seasonal vegetables and lightly buttered egg noodles sprinkled with chopped fresh parsley. The wine and whipping cream in the sauce make the cutlets extremely rich and luscious — serve them on an occasion that calls for such a dish.

ERIC'S OPTIONS
Prepare this dish with boneless, skinless chicken breasts or turkey cutlets instead of pork cutlets.

3/4 cup	all-purpose flour	175 mL
2 Tbsp.	olive oil	25 mL
8	3-oz. (75-g) boneless pork cutlets	8
to taste	salt and freshly cracked black pepper	to taste
1 cup	white wine	250 mL
1 1/2 cups	whipping cream	375 mL
1/3 cup	grainy Dijon mustard	75 mL
2 Tbsp.	chopped fresh parsley or chives	25 mL

Place the flour on a plate. Heat the oil in a skillet over medium-high heat. While the oil is heating, season the pork with salt and pepper and then dredge the cutlets in the flour, shaking off the excess. Add the pork to the skillet and cook for 2–3 minutes per side, or until just cooked through.

Remove from the pan and set aside. Remove the excess fat from the pan. Add the wine to the pan and cook until it's reduced by half. Add the cream and cook until the sauce slightly thickens. Stir in the mustard and parsley or chives. Season with salt and pepper to taste. Return the pork to the pan and heat through. Serve the pork cutlets on individual plates and spoon the sauce over top.

Monterey Jack and   140
Jalapeño Cornbread

Blue Cheese Biscuits   141

Speedy Salsa   142

Quick Rouille   143

Tzatziki Sauce   144

Orzo Baked with Green   145
Onions and Parmesan

Balsamic Roasted Asparagus   146

ON THE SIDE

CHAPTER NINE

Carrots with Honey,   147
Ginger and Lemon

Glazed Yams with   148
Cranberries and Pecans

Brussels Sprouts Stir-Fried   150
with Red Onions and Peppers

Buttermilk Yukon Gold   151
Mashed Potatoes

Roasted New Potatoes   152
with Lemon and Dijon

MONTEREY JACK and JALAPEÑO CORNBREAD

preparation time · 20 minutes
cooking time · 45 minutes
makes · 2 loaves

Serve this spicy cornbread with Chunky Chili with Dark Ale (page 122).

ERIC'S OPTIONS
If you can't take the heat, substitute half a medium green bell pepper, finely chopped, for the jalapeño, or simply omit.

2 cups	cornmeal	500 mL
2 cups	all-purpose flour	500 mL
1/2 cup	sugar	125 mL
1 tsp.	salt	5 mL
2 Tbsp.	baking powder	25 mL
2 1/2 cups	milk	625 mL
2	large eggs, beaten	2
1/2 cup	vegetable oil	125 mL
2–3	jalapeño peppers, fresh or canned (drained well), finely chopped	2–3
1 cup	grated Monterey Jack cheese	250 mL

Preheat the oven to 350°F (180°C). Lightly grease 2 non-stick loaf pans with butter or vegetable spray. Combine the cornmeal, flour, sugar, salt and baking powder in a bowl. In another bowl, mix the remaining ingredients. Add the wet ingredients to the dry until just combined. (The batter will be quite wet.) Spoon into the pans. Bake for 45 minutes, or until a toothpick inserted into the centre of each loaf comes out clean. Cool in the pans for a few minutes, then carefully unmould onto a baking rack.

BLUE CHEESE BISCUITS

preparation time · 15–20 minutes
cooking time · 12–15 minutes
makes · 12–15 biscuits

These biscuits are great to serve with stews and braised dishes, such as Southern-Style Short Ribs (page 114).

ERIC'S OPTIONS
Instead of green onions use 1–2 Tbsp. (15–25 mL) of fresh chopped herbs, such as parsley, chives or rosemary. For plain biscuits omit the green onions and blue cheese.

2 cups	flour	500 mL
1/2 tsp.	salt	2 mL
1/2 tsp.	baking soda	2 mL
2 tsp.	baking powder	10 mL
1 tsp.	sugar	5 mL
1/4 cup	butter	50 mL
1/3 cup	crumbled blue cheese	75 mL
2	green onions, finely chopped	2
1 1/4 cups	buttermilk	300 mL

Preheat the oven to 425°F (220°C). Sift the flour, salt, baking soda, baking powder and sugar into a bowl. With your fingers or a fork, cut in the butter until the mixture forms pea-sized crumbles. Mix in the cheese and green onions. Gently mix in the buttermilk until a loose dough forms. Turn the dough onto a floured surface and shape into a ball. Flatten into a disc 3/4 inch (2 cm) thick. Cut into 2-inch (5-cm) rounds and place on a baking sheet. Bake in the middle of the oven for 12–15 minutes, until puffed and golden.

SPEEDY SALSA

preparation time ·	10 minutes	
cooking time ·	none	
makes ·	about 3 cups (750 mL)	

This fresh-tasting salsa has a much crunchier texture and livelier flavour than store-bought, which is fully cooked before it's sealed in jars. Making this in a food processor reduces the time-consuming task of finely chopping the vegetables.

ERIC'S OPTIONS
For a mild-tasting salsa use only half a jalapeño pepper. For a really fresh taste, substitute 1 2/3 cups (400 mL) chopped fresh tomatoes for the canned.

1	medium green bell pepper, seeded and cut into chunks	1
1/2	medium red onion, cut into chunks	1/2
1–2	jalapeño peppers, coarsely chopped	1–2
1/4 cup	coarsely chopped fresh cilantro	50 mL
2–3	limes, juiced	2–3
1	14–oz. (398–mL) can diced tomatoes	1
pinch	sugar	pinch
to taste	salt	to taste

Place the bell pepper, onion, jalapeño peppers, cilantro and lime juice in a food processor. Pulse in short spurts until the vegetables resemble a small dice. Transfer the processed vegetables to a bowl and stir in the remaining ingredients. Salsa can be refrigerated in a tightly sealed container for 1 week but is at its best shortly after it's made.

QUICK
ROUILLE

preparation time · 5 minutes
cooking time · none
makes · 1¼ cups (300 mL)

Rather than pounding the ingredients together as is traditionally done, my quick version of this classic sauce is blended in a food processor.

ERIC'S OPTIONS
Although this sauce is traditionally served with bouillabaisse (see Canadian-Style Bouillabaisse, page 72), it makes a nice dip for raw vegetable sticks or grilled prawns. It is also a fine spread for sandwiches, particularly those filled with grilled or roasted vegetables and/or Mediterranean-style meats and cheeses.

1	roasted red bell pepper (see page 13), sliced	1
2	garlic cloves, coarsely chopped	2
1	slice white bread, torn into pieces	1
¾ cup	mayonnaise	175 mL
to taste	salt, freshly cracked black pepper, cayenne pepper and lemon juice	to taste

Place all the ingredients in a food processor and process until smooth. Place in a bowl, cover, and allow the flavours to meld in the refrigerator for several hours.

TZATZIKI
SAUCE

preparation time	·	10 minutes
cooking time	·	none
makes	·	1 1/4 cups (300 mL)

Serve this Greek-style sauce with filo-wrapped savouries, grilled meats, kebabs, pita or raw vegetable sticks.

ERIC'S OPTIONS
If you don't have fresh herbs, sub-stitute 1/2 tsp. (2 mL) dried.

1/2 cup	yogurt	125 mL
1/4 cup	sour cream	50 mL
1/2	English cucumber, coarsely grated and moisture squeezed out	1/2
2	garlic cloves, chopped	2
1 Tbsp.	chopped fresh dill	15 mL
1 Tbsp.	chopped fresh mint	15 mL
to taste	salt, freshly cracked black pepper and lemon juice	to taste

Combine all the ingredients in a bowl. Cover and allow the flavours to meld in the refrigerator for several hours before serving.

ORZO BAKED with GREEN ONIONS and PARMESAN

preparation time · 10 minutes
cooking time · 30–40 minutes
makes · 4–6 servings

Orzo is a pasta shaped like rice with an interesting texture lieing somewhere between the two. Serve this side dish as a sauce catcher for stews and braised dishes.

ERIC'S OPTIONS
Add chopped or sliced vegetables, such as tinned artichokes, sun-dried tomatoes, olives, roasted peppers or cooked mushrooms, to the orzo before baking.

1½ cups	orzo	375 mL
1	bunch green onions, chopped	1
3	garlic cloves, chopped	3
1 cup	freshly grated Parmesan cheese	250 mL
3 Tbsp.	olive oil	45 mL
to taste	salt and freshly cracked black pepper	to taste
¾ cups	chicken or vegetable stock	175 mL

Preheat the oven to 350°F (180°C). Cook the orzo according to package directions. Drain well, chill in cold water, drain well again and place in a bowl. Mix in the onions (reserving a few for garnish), garlic, ¾ cup (175 mL) of the cheese, oil, salt and pepper. Spoon into a lightly oiled casserole dish. Pour in the stock. Top with the remaining ¼ cup (50 mL) cheese. Cover and bake for 30–40 minutes, or until heated through. Sprinkle with the reserved green onions before serving.

BALSAMIC ROASTED ASPARAGUS

preparation time · 10 minutes
cooking time · 20–25 minutes
makes · 4 servings

As the asparagus roasts, the balsamic vinegar thickens and caramelizes around the spears, infusing them with a slightly sweet, slightly tart flavour. Serve the asparagus alongside roasted or grilled meats, chicken or fish.

ERIC'S OPTIONS
I like to serve this dish at room temperature in the summer. Make it without the Parmesan cheese in the morning, cool it to room temperature and store it in the refrigerator. Warm it to room temperature 30 minutes before transferring to a serving platter, spooning the pan juices over top and sprinkling with the cheese.

1 lb.	asparagus	500 g
1/4 cup	balsamic vinegar	50 mL
2 Tbsp.	olive oil	25 mL
to taste	salt and freshly cracked black pepper	to taste
1/4 cup	grated Parmesan cheese	50 mL

Preheat the oven to 400°F (200°C). Bring a large pot of water to a rapid boil. Snap the ends off the asparagus and discard or save them to flavour soup stock. Cook the asparagus in the boiling water for 1 minute. Drain well, chill in cold water and drain well again. Place the asparagus in a casserole dish and drizzle with the vinegar and oil. Sprinkle with salt, pepper and cheese. Roast for 20–25 minutes and serve immediately with the pan juices.

CARROTS with HONEY, GINGER and LEMON

preparation time · 5 minutes
cooking time · 7–8 minutes
makes · 4–6 servings

Honey, ginger and a touch of lemon give plain old carrots an intriguing, slightly sweet, spicy and sour taste.

ERIC'S OPTIONS
Use 1 lb. (500 g) of baby carrots instead of carrot sticks. Carrots can be cooked ahead, drained well, cooled in ice water, drained well again and stored in the refrigerator. Reheat in the butter mixture later. Add 1/4 cup (50 mL) of cold water to the skillet when you do so, as they will take a few minutes to heat through, and require this added moisture.

3	medium carrots, peeled and cut into sticks	3
2 Tbsp.	butter	25 mL
1 tsp.	freshly grated ginger, or to taste	5 mL
1 Tbsp.	liquid honey, or to taste	15 mL
1 Tbsp.	lemon juice	15 mL
to taste	salt and freshly cracked black pepper	to taste
1 Tbsp.	chopped fresh parsley or chives	15 mL

Place the carrots in a pot, cover with cold water and boil until just tender. Melt the butter in a skillet over medium heat. Add the ginger, honey and lemon juice and mix to combine. Drain the carrots well and add them to the skillet. Add the salt, pepper, parsley or chives and toss to combine. Serve immediately.

GLAZED YAMS with CRANBERRIES and PECANS

preparation time	·	20 minutes
cooking time	·	80–90 minutes (includes pre-cooking the yams)
makes	·	8 servings

Here's a rich-tasting side dish that can be readied hours in advance and baked later. This makes it a good item for a holiday dinner: it will be ready to go when your guests arrive, allowing you to spend more time with them, rather than in the kitchen.

ERIC'S OPTIONS
Use 2–3 Tbsp. (25–45 mL) of slightly warmed maple syrup or liquid honey instead of brown sugar. This will give the yams a shinier look and a slightly sweeter taste.

6	medium yams (see next page)	6
1/3 cup	fresh or frozen cranberries (thawed), coarsely chopped	75 mL
1/3 cup	pecan pieces	75 mL
3–4 Tbsp.	butter, at room temperature	45–60 mL
to taste	salt and freshly cracked black pepper	to taste
1/4 cup	brown sugar	50 mL
1/2 tsp.	ground cinnamon	2 mL
pinch	ground nutmeg	pinch

Preheat the oven to 350°F (180°C). Prick the yams several times with a fork. Place on a baking sheet and bake until tender but still slightly firm, about 60 minutes, depending on the size. Remove and set aside until cool enough to handle.

When still warm, carefully remove the skin with a small knife. Slice the yams into 3/4-inch (2-cm) thick rounds and place in slightly overlapping rows in a lightly buttered 9 x 13-inch (23 x 33-cm) baking dish. Scatter the cranberries and pecans overtop. Melt the remaining butter and drizzle over the top. Season with salt and pepper. Combine the sugar, cinnamon and nutmeg in a small bowl. Sprinkle the mixture over the yams. (The dish could be made to this point several hours in advance and stored in the refrigerator until needed.) Bake for 20–30 minutes, or until the yams are heated through and nicely glazed.

SWEET POTATOES AND YAMS

You'll find sweet potatoes and yams for sale in most mainstream supermarkets. However, most often those yams are actually the orange-fleshed variety of sweet potato. True yams, a staple ingredient in many Asian countries, are much larger than sweet potatoes and can grow up to 3 feet (90 cm) long. While sweet potatoes can be cooked in their skin and the skin eaten, the skin of a true yam must be deeply peeled before cooking and is never eaten because it contains irritating crystals of calcium oxalate.

Why, you may wonder, is the orange-fleshed variety of sweet potato called a yam in North America? It was a marketing ploy designed to help consumers distinguish it from the other sweet potato, which has a pale yellow flesh and pale brown skin. The skin of the orange-fleshed vegetable is most often a copper colour and its flesh is moist, dense and quite sweet. The yellow-fleshed variety is dryer in texture, less sweet and has an almost nutty flavour.

The two varieties are suited to different preparations. If you are looking for a sweet potato to use in a salad or casserole, one that will hold its shape when cooked, the orange-fleshed variety is best. The yellow-fleshed variety, which has a starchy character like that of a baking potato, is best eaten as you would a potato — baked whole; cut into wedges, tossed with oil and spices and roasted; or peeled, boiled, mashed and mixed with buttermilk, butter and salt and pepper.

In this book, in line with common practice, the orange-fleshed sweet potato is referred to as a yam.

BRUSSELS SPROUTS STIR-FRIED
with RED ONIONS and PEPPERS

preparation time · 20 minutes
cooking time · 10–12 minutes
makes · 4–6 servings

I serve this colourful dish at Thanksgiving or Christmas, but it is an attractive side dish for any fall or winter dinner. The vegetables can be readied hours in advance and refrigerated until you are ready to stir-fry.

ERIC'S OPTIONS
If you're just not a fan of Brussels sprouts, replace them with broccoli or cauliflower florets.

1 lb.	Brussels sprouts, trimmed and halved if large	500 g
2 Tbsp.	vegetable oil	25 mL
1/2	small red onion, finely chopped	1/2
1/2	medium yellow bell pepper, seeded and finely chopped	1/2
1/2	medium red bell pepper, seeded and finely chopped	1/2
2 tsp.	chopped fresh ginger	10 mL
1/4 cup	chicken stock or water	50 mL
2-3 Tbsp.	chopped fresh parsley	25–45 mL
to taste	salt and freshly cracked black pepper	to taste

Boil or steam the Brussels sprouts until firm-tender. Drain well, chill in cold water, drain well again and set aside.

Heat the oil in a skillet over medium-high heat. Add the onion, peppers and ginger and stir-fry for 2 minutes. Add the Brussels sprouts and stir-fry for 2 minutes more. Add the stock or water and cook until it has almost evaporated and the Brussels sprouts are tender. Sprinkle in the parsley, season with salt and pepper, and serve.

BUTTERMILK YUKON GOLD MASHED POTATOES

preparation time · 5 minutes
cooking time · 20 minutes
makes · 4–6 servings

The eye-appealing colour and texture of Yukon Gold potatoes make them my favourite for mashing. Buttermilk gives them an added tanginess. These mashed potatoes go well with a range of dishes, from baked salmon to meatloaf or roast chicken.

ERIC'S OPTIONS
Substitute freshly chopped chives for the green onions. To make Italian-style mashed potatoes, flavour the potatoes with a little truffle oil and whip in 1/4 cup (50 mL) of freshly grated Parmesan cheese. For saffron mashed potatoes, add 1/2 tsp. (2 mL) saffron threads to the potatoes before you start boiling them.

2 1/2 lbs.	Yukon Gold potatoes, peeled and halved	1.1 kg
3/4 cup	warm buttermilk	175 ml
2 Tbsp.	melted butter	25 mL
1/4 cup	chopped green onions	50 mL
to taste	salt and freshly cracked black pepper	to taste

Gently boil the potatoes until tender. Drain well and thoroughly mash. Whip in the remaining ingredients until well combined and the mixture is lightened.

You can make the potatoes up to a day in advance and reheat them in the oven. Spoon the prepared mixture into a lightly buttered casserole. Cool to room temperature, cover and refrigerate. At serving time, brush the top with a little melted butter and bake in a 350°F (175°C) oven for 30 minutes, until the potatoes are heated through and golden on top.

ROASTED NEW POTATOES
with LEMON and DIJON

preparation time · 10 minutes
cooking time · 40 minutes
makes · 6–8 servings

These potatoes make a fine side dish for almost any kind of roast and are especially good with lamb and poached or baked salmon. They can be made oven-ready hours in advance and roasted later.

ERIC'S OPTIONS
Use other chopped herbs, such as thyme or sage, or a mix of herbs, instead of rosemary. Replace the fresh rosemary with 1 tsp. (5 mL) dried. If you like garlic, add 3–4 thinly sliced garlic cloves to the potatoes before roasting.

3 lbs.	small new red or white potatoes, washed well and cut in half	1.5 kg
3 Tbsp.	olive oil	45 mL
to taste	salt and freshly cracked black pepper	to taste
1	grated zest and juice of lemon	1
1/3 cup	grainy Dijon mustard	75 mL
1 Tbsp.	chopped fresh rosemary	15 mL

Preheat the oven to 400°F (200°C). Boil the potatoes until firm-tender. Drain well and place in a bowl. Add the remaining ingredients and gently toss. Place the potatoes in a single layer on a baking tray. (Cover and refrigerate now if roasting them later.) Roast for 30–40 minutes, turning once halfway through the cooking to ensure even browning, until golden brown and slightly crispy around the edges.

Chewy Oatmeal   154
Cranberry Cookies

Whipped Shortbread   156

Pantry Cookies   158

Chocolate Macadamia   159
Nut Shortbread

Devie's Maple Pecan   160
Butter Cookies

A JAR FULL OF COOKIES

CHAPTER TEN

Chocolate Lover's   161
Cookies

Almond Cranberry   162
Biscotti

Annette's Swedish   164
Pepparkakor

Meringue Kisses   165

CHEWY OATMEAL CRANBERRY COOKIES

preparation time · 20 minutes
cooking time · 12–15 minutes
makes · 24–30 cookies

Dried, slightly tart cranberries make these chewy oatmeal cookies less sweet than those made with raisins.

ERIC'S OPTIONS
Use 3/4 cup (175 mL) raisins or chocolate chips, or a mix of both, instead of dried cranberries.

1 cup	butter, at room temperature	250 mL
1 cup	golden brown sugar, packed	250 mL
1/2 cup	granulated sugar	125 mL
2	large eggs	2
1 tsp.	vanilla extract	5 mL
1 tsp.	ground cinnamon	5 mL
1/2 tsp.	salt	2 mL
1/2 tsp.	baking soda	2 mL
1 1/4 cups	all-purpose flour	300 mL
3 cups	quick-cooking oats	750 mL
3/4 cup	dried cranberries	175 mL

Preheat the oven to 350°F (180°C). Beat the butter and both sugars until light. Beat in the eggs one at a time. Add the vanilla and mix well. Place the remaining ingredients in another bowl and mix until well combined. Gradually mix the dry mixture into the butter mixture until well combined. Use a 2-Tbsp. (25-mL) measure to drop spoonfuls of batter onto non-stick or parchment-lined cookie sheets, leaving a 2- to 3-inch (5- to 8-cm) space between each cookie. Bake for 12–15 minutes. Place the sheets on a rack and allow the cookies to completely cool before removing and storing in a tightly sealed jar or tin.

LEARNING TO MEASURE

There are many things one can learn about baking, but the first should be learning how to measure. Most baking recipes are like scientific formulas and things can go awry if you're not accurate. Measurements should be level, not almost full or heaped up. For cup, tablespoon or teaspoon measurements of dry ingredients, use tools designed for this task; they hold only the correct amount needed. When using cup and spoon measures for dry ingredients, run a flat edge, such as the side of a knife, a pastry scraper or thin spatula across the top of the measure to remove any excess. For liquids, use glass measuring cups that have extra room at the top so the liquid won't spill out when you transfer it to the mixing bowl. Place the cup on the counter when measuring; holding it in your hand can give an inaccurate measurement.

PURCHASING AND STORING NUTS

When using nuts in cookies or any other recipe make sure they are fresh. Nuts that are even slightly off will impart a strong, unappealing taste and smell to whatever you are making. Nuts have a high oil content that can cause them to go rancid relatively quickly. Purchase them from a retailer that has a high rate of turnover. To keep them fresh, store them in a tightly sealed container in the refrigerator for up to four months or in the freezer for up to six months.

WHIPPED SHORTBREAD

preparation time · 20–30 minutes
cooking time · 12–18 minutes
makes · 48–60 cookies, depending on the size

Unlike traditional shortbread recipes, this dough is pliable, making it easy to shape and use in a variety of ways. You can make an assortment of shortbread from one batch of dough by dividing it in two or three pieces and following the shaping and flavouring suggestions (see next page).

3 cups	all-purpose flour	750 mL
1/2 cup	cornstarch	125 mL
1/2 tsp.	salt	2 mL
1 lb.	butter, at room temperature	500 g
1 cup	icing sugar	250 mL
1 tsp.	vanilla extract	5 mL

Preheat the oven to 325°F (160°C). Sift the flour, cornstarch and salt together in a bowl. In a separate bowl, cream the butter and sugar until quite light. Mix in the vanilla. Gradually add the flour mixture and beat until smooth. Pipe or shape the cookies as suggested on the next page. Place on non-stick or parchment-lined cookie sheets, spacing them about 1 inch (2.5 cm) apart. Bake until very pale golden in colour, about 12–18 minutes depending on the thickness. Place the sheets on a rack and allow the cookies to completely cool before removing and storing in a tightly sealed jar or tin.

ROLLED AND DECORATED
Chill the dough for 30 minutes. Roll out on a lightly floured surface to
1/4 inch (5 mm) thick. Use cookie cutters to create various shapes. Before
baking decorate, if desired, with whole or half nuts, silver balls, coloured
sugar, chocolate chips, candies or candied fruit.

PIPED
Place the dough in a piping bag fitted with a large star tip. Pipe into small
rounds or fingers. Chill for 20 minutes before baking. If desired, make a small
indentation in the centre of the rounds before baking and fill with jam or jelly
after baking. Or dip one end of each finger in melted chocolate after baking.

RUM AND CURRANT
Soak 1/2 cup (125 mL) currants in rum overnight. Drain well. (Reserve the rum
for another use, such as Rum-Glazed Fresh Pineapple Rings, page 168). Mix
the currants into half the shortbread dough. Roll into small balls and bake.
If desired, coat in icing sugar, cocoa or cinnamon sugar when cool.

CHOCOLATE CHIP
Mix 1/2 cup (125 mL) semisweet chocolate chips into half the shortbread dough.
Proceed as for rum and currant shortbread.

NUT CRESCENTS
Mix 1/2 cup (125 mL) finely chopped nuts, such as pecans, walnuts or hazelnuts,
into half the shortbread dough. Lightly flour your hands and form the dough into
small crescent shapes. When baked and cooled, dust with icing sugar or cocoa.

PANTRY
COOKIES

preparation time ·	20–25 minutes
cooking time ·	12–15 minutes
makes ·	48 cookies

These cookies are so named because just about everything in my pantry, except flour, went into making them. Serve them warm with a glass of ice-cold milk.

ERIC'S OPTIONS
Replace the chips, currants and walnuts with an equal amount of whatever you have in your pantry, such as raisins, dried cranberries or chopped pecans.

1/2 cup	butter	125 mL
1 1/3 cups	peanut butter	325 mL
1 1/4 cups	golden brown sugar, packed	300 mL
1 cup	granulated sugar	250 mL
3	large eggs	3
1 tsp.	vanilla extract	5 mL
4 cups	quick-cooking oats	1 L
2 tsp.	baking soda	10 mL
1/2 cup	semisweet chocolate chips	125 mL
1/2 cup	caramel chips	125 mL
1/2 cup	currants	125 mL
1/2 cup	chopped walnuts	125 mL

Preheat the oven to 350°F (180°C). Beat the butter, peanut butter and both sugars until light. Mix in the eggs one at a time. Add the vanilla and mix well. Combine the oats and baking soda in a bowl and stir into the batter. Mix in the remaining ingredients. Using a 2-Tbsp. (25-mL) measure, roll the dough into balls and place on non-stick or parchment-lined cookie sheets, gently pressing them down. Leave a 2- to 3-inch (5- to 8-cm) space between each cookie. Bake for 12–15 minutes. Place the sheets on a rack and allow the cookies to completely cool before removing and storing in a tightly sealed jar or tin.

CHOCOLATE MACADAMIA NUT SHORTBREAD

preparation time · 20 minutes
cooking time · 25–30 minutes
makes · 24–30 cookies

Brown sugar gives these rich cookies an even richer flavour.

NOTE
Blanched macadamia nuts are sold in most supermarkets along with the other nuts.

ERIC'S OPTIONS
Whole blanched almonds or walnut or pecan halves could replace the macadamia nuts.

1 cup	butter, at room temperature	250 mL
1/2 cup	brown sugar, packed	125 mL
1 tsp.	vanilla extract	5 mL
1 1/2 cups	all-purpose flour	375 mL
1/2 cup	chocolate chips	125 mL
24–30	blanched macadamia nuts	24–30

Preheat the oven to 300°F (150°C). Beat the butter, sugar and vanilla until light. Add the flour and mix just until the dough begins to hold together. Mix in the chocolate chips. Roll the dough into 1 1/2- to 2-inch (4- to 5-cm) balls and place on non-stick or parchment-lined cookie sheets, spacing them about 1–2 inches (2.5–5 cm) apart. With your finger, make a small indentation in the middle of each cookie. Insert a macadamia nut into the indentation. Bake the cookies for 25–30 minutes, or until they are very light golden brown. Place the sheets on a rack and allow the cookies to completely cool before storing in a tightly sealed jar or tin.

DEVIE'S MAPLE PECAN BUTTER COOKIES

preparation time · 25–30 minutes
cooking time · 12–15 minutes
makes · 8 dozen small cookies

This cookie recipe comes from a food-loving friend and baker extraordinaire. It's a good thing these cookies are small as it is impossible to just have one!

ERIC'S OPTIONS
Once shaped into logs, this dough freezes well. Thaw until soft enough to slice.

1/2 lb.	butter	250 g
1/2 cup	granulated sugar	125 mL
1	large egg yolk	1
2 Tbsp.	maple syrup	25 mL
1/2 tsp.	vanilla extract	2 mL
1 7/8 cups	all-purpose flour	475 mL
1 1/4 cups	finely chopped pecans	300 mL

Beat the butter until light. Beat in the sugar until well-blended. Mix in the egg yolk, maple syrup and vanilla. Add the flour and nuts and mix until just combined. Wrap the dough in plastic wrap and chill for 30 minutes. Divide the dough into 4 pieces and roll them into 2-inch-thick (5-cm) logs. Wrap and chill the logs until firm enough to slice, about 30 minutes.

Preheat the oven to 325°F (160°C). Slice the logs into 1/4-inch (5-mm) rounds and place on non-stick or parchment-lined cookie sheets, spacing them 1–2 inches (2.5–5 cm) apart. Bake for 12–15 minutes. Place the sheets on a rack and allow the cookies to completely cool before removing and storing in a tightly sealed jar or tin.

Carrots with Honey, Ginger and Lemon, 147;
Roasted New Potatoes with Lemon and Dijon, 152;
Brussels Sprouts Stir-Fried with Red Onions and Peppers, 150

Monterey Jack and Jalapeño Cornbread, 140; Blue Cheese Biscuits, 141

Steamed Cranberry
and Raisin Pudding, 174

Whipped
Shortbread, 156;
Chocolate
Macadamia Nut
Shortbread, 159

Rum-Glazed Fresh
Pineapple Rings, 168

Almond
Cranberry
Biscotti, 162

Devie's Maple
Pecan Butter
Cookies, 160

Strawberries in
Sparkling Wine
with Honey
Whipped
Cream, 169

CHOCOLATE LOVER'S COOKIES

preparation time ·	20–25 minutes
cooking time ·	20 minutes
makes ·	6 large cookies

Lots of chocolate, a fair amount of sugar and almost no flour gives these cookies a dense, meringue-like quality. With a crisp exterior and a moist middle that melts in your mouth, these are a chocolate lover's dream!

ERIC'S OPTIONS
For a less sweet cookie, substitute bitter chocolate for 1/2 of the semisweet. To make a plated dessert, set a cookie on a dessert plate, top with a scoop of vanilla ice cream, drizzle with a little melted chocolate or chocolate sauce, top with a few fresh berries, and garnish with mint.

4 oz.	semisweet chocolate, coarsely chopped	125 g
3 Tbsp.	butter	45 mL
1 tsp.	instant coffee granules	5 mL
2 Tbsp.	all-purpose flour	25 mL
1/4 tsp.	baking powder	1 mL
1/4 tsp.	salt	1 mL
1	large egg	1
1/3 cup	sugar	75 mL
1 tsp.	vanilla extract	5 mL
1/3 cup	dark chocolate chips	75 mL
1/3 cup	white chocolate chips	75 mL
1/3 cup	pecan halves	75 mL

Preheat the oven to 300°F (150°C). Melt the chocolate and butter in a heatproof bowl set over simmering water. Remove from the heat, stir in coffee granules, and cool to just above room temperature.

Combine the flour, baking powder and salt in a small bowl. In another bowl, beat the egg and sugar until very light. Beat in the melted chocolate and vanilla. Add the flour mixture and stir just until combined. Stir in the chocolate chips and pecans. Using a 1/4–1/3 cup (60–80 mL) measure, drop the batter about 3 inches (8 cm) apart on a parchment-lined cookie sheet. Bake for 20 minutes, until the tops begin to crack slightly. Place the baking sheet on a rack and let the cookies completely cool before removing.

ALMOND CRANBERRY BISCOTTI

preparation time	·	40 minutes
cooking time	·	40 minutes
makes	·	24–30 cookies

These crunchy cookies are great for dunking in coffee or tea.

ERIC'S OPTIONS
Substitute unsalted, shelled pistachios for the almonds. Coarsely chop them before adding them to the dough. Use dried blueberries, raisins or currants instead of dried cranberries.

1/3 cup	butter	75 mL
3/4 cup	sugar	175 mL
2	eggs	2
1/2 tsp.	almond extract	2 mL
1/2 tsp.	vanilla extract	2 mL
1 tsp.	grated orange zest	5 mL
2 1/4 cups	all-purpose flour	550 mL
2 tsp.	baking powder	10 mL
1/4 tsp.	salt	1 mL
1/2 cup	whole almonds, lightly toasted (see page 24) and coarsely chopped	125 mL
1/4 cup	dried cranberries	50 mL
1	large egg white, beaten	1
	sugar for sprinkling on top	

Preheat the oven to 350°F (180°C). Beat the butter and sugar until light. Beat in the eggs, extracts and orange zest. Sift the flour with the baking powder and salt. Beat the dry mixture into the butter mixture. Mix in the almonds and cranberries. Divide the dough in half and place on a lightly floured work surface. Shape and knead each half into a smooth, oval-shaped log about 12 inches (30 cm) long and $2^{1}/_{2}$ inches (6 cm) wide. Place the logs on a large, non-stick or parchment-lined baking sheet. Brush the tops with beaten egg white and sprinkle with a little sugar. Bake for 20 minutes, or until a light golden brown.

Carefully lift from the baking sheet and cool on a rack for 5 minutes. Carefully lift from the rack and place on a cutting board. With a serrated knife, slice the logs on a slight diagonal into $^{1}/_{2}$-inch (1-cm) slices. Lay the slices flat on the baking sheet. Return to the oven and bake for 10 minutes. Turn and bake for 10 minutes more. Cool the cookies completely on a baking rack. Store in a tightly covered container for up to 3 weeks.

ANNETTE'S SWEDISH PEPPARKAKOR

preparation time ·	40–50 minutes	
cooking time ·	10–12 minutes	
makes ·	6–7 dozen small cookies	

This traditional Scandinavian-style ginger cookie gets better with age. I recommend a week or two in a tightly sealed container, but in my house these tasty cookies never seem to stay around that long.

ERIC'S OPTIONS
This dough freezes well. Thaw it in the fridge overnight before using.

1 cup	butter, at room temperature	250 mL
1/2 cup	molasses	125 mL
3 cups	all-purpose flour	750 mL
1 cup	sugar	250 mL
2 tsp.	baking soda	10 mL
1 tsp.	ground cardamom	5 mL
1 tsp.	ground ginger	5 mL
1 tsp.	ground cloves	5 mL
1 tsp.	ground cinnamon	5 mL
1	large egg, beaten	1
3 Tbsp.	milk	45 mL

In a small pot over low heat, melt the butter and molasses, stirring to combine. In a large bowl combine the flour, sugar, baking soda, cardamom, ginger, cloves and cinnamon. Add the butter mixture, egg and milk. Beat with an electric mixer or by hand until well combined. The dough will appear quite moist. Place the dough on a large sheet of plastic wrap, flatten, securely wrap it and refrigerate overnight.

Preheat the oven to 350°F (180°C). Divide the dough into quarters. Working with one quarter at a time (keep the others refrigerated), roll the dough on a lightly floured work surface to 1/8 inch (3 mm) thick. Using cookie cutters, cut the dough into shapes and place on a parchment-lined cookie sheet, spacing them 1 inch (2.5 cm) apart. Bake for 10–12 minutes. Place the baking sheets on a rack and allow the cookies to completely cool before storing in a tightly sealed jar or tin.

MERINGUE KISSES

preparation time · 20 minutes
cooking time · 2½ hours
makes · about 3 dozen, depending on size

These light, dreamy cookies are splendid additions to any festive cookie tray.

ERIC'S OPTIONS
For chocolate chip meringue kisses, place chocolate chips at various points around the outside of the piped or mounded meringue before baking. The mixture can also be shaped in other ways. Make small meringue shells, good for filling with jam, ice cream or whipped cream and fruit, by piping or mounding meringue in 2- to 3-inch (5- to 8-cm) circles, building the edges up to create a pocket in the middle. Remember, the thinner your meringue is, the less baking time it will require.

4	large egg whites	4
½ tsp.	cream of tartar	2 mL
1 cup	extra fine (berry) sugar	250 mL

Preheat the oven to 225°F (105°C). Line a cookie sheet with parchment paper. Beat the egg whites and cream of tartar together until very soft peaks form. Add the sugar 1 Tbsp. (15 mL) at a time, beating constantly. Keep beating until the mixture is thick and glossy and stiff peaks form.

Spoon the meringue into a piping bag fitted with a star tip and pipe into rosettes that are about 1 inch (2.5 cm) across and 2 inches (5 cm) high. If you don't have a piping bag, simply spoon the mixture into fluffy mounds of a similar size. Bake for 20 minutes, or until dry and crisp on the outside and slightly chewy in the middle. (The meringues should be quite white; if they appear to be browning during baking, reduce the heat to 200°F/95°C.) Turn the oven off and let the meringues cool completely in the oven. This should take about 2 hours.

Meringue kisses will keep for several weeks in an airtight container at room temperature or in the freezer. They must be stored in a single layer, not stacked.

Rum-Glazed Fresh   168
Pineapple Rings

Strawberries in Sparkling Wine   169
with Honey Whipped Cream

Champagne Sabayon   170

Pinot Noir   171
Poached Pears

Blackberry and   172
Apple Pie

Pastry for a Double   173
Pie Crust

DIVINE

DESSERTS

CHAPTER ELEVEN

Steamed Cranberry   174
and Raisin Pudding

Chocolate Fondue   176
for Two

Hot Brownie Pudding   177

Luscious Lemon Cake   178

Creamy Coffee   179
Cheesecake

RUM-GLAZED FRESH PINEAPPLE RINGS

preparation time · 10 minutes
cooking time · 15–20 minutes
makes · 4 servings

Rum, butter and spice combine to make fresh pineapple more splendid than it already is.

ERIC'S OPTIONS
To enhance the tropical taste, try ginger or macadamia nut ice cream.

4	slices peeled and cored fresh pineapple, cut 1¹/₂ inches (4 cm) thick	4
2 Tbsp.	melted butter	25 mL
1	lime, juiced	1
2 oz.	dark rum	50 mL
¹/₂ cup	brown sugar, lightly packed	125 mL
¹/₄ tsp.	ground nutmeg	1 mL
¹/₂ tsp.	ground cinnamon	2 mL
4	scoops vanilla ice cream	4
	fresh mint sprigs	

Preheat the oven to 450°F (230°C). Place the pineapple rings in a single layer in a shallow baking dish just large enough to hold them. Combine the butter, lime juice and rum in a small bowl. Spoon over the pineapple. Combine the brown sugar, nutmeg and cinnamon in a small bowl, then sprinkle over the pineapple. Bake for 15–20 minutes, until the pineapple is glazed and just tender. Place the pineapple rings on dessert plates and spoon the pan juices over top. Place a scoop of vanilla ice cream in the middle of each ring. Garnish with fresh mint sprigs and serve immediately.

STRAWBERRIES in SPARKLING WINE with HONEY WHIPPED CREAM

preparation time · 15 minutes
cooking time · none
makes · 4 servings

Here's a simple dessert that's at its best when local strawberries are in season.

ERIC'S OPTIONS
Try combining sliced strawberries with whole berries such as rasp-berries, blueberries and blackberries.

4 cups	sliced strawberries	1 L
1 cup	sparkling wine	250 mL
1/2 cup	whipping cream	125 mL
to taste	liquid honey	to taste
	fresh mint sprigs	

Place the strawberries in a bowl. Add the sparkling wine. Cover with plastic wrap and let stand for 30 minutes. Whip the whipping cream until soft peaks form. Flavour with honey, then beat until stiff peaks form. Spoon the strawberries into serving glasses (champagne flutes are ideal). Top with whipped cream and garnish with mint sprigs.

CHAMPAGNE SABAYON

preparation time · 5 minutes
cooking time · 10 minutes
makes · 2 servings

This classic French dessert will bring a light, sweet ending to a romantic meal.

ERIC'S OPTIONS
For an orange-scented sabayon, replace 1/4 of the Champagne with orange liqueur, such as Grand Marnier.

2	large egg yolks, at room temperature	2
1/4 cup	granulated sugar	50 mL
1/4 cup	Champagne or other sparkling wine	50 mL
	mint sprigs	
	ladyfingers and strawberries	

Place the egg yolks, sugar and wine in a medium-sized heatproof bowl. Beat with a thin wire whisk until very light and foamy. Place the bowl over, not in, simmering water. Continue beating until the mixture becomes almost as thick as whipped cream, greatly increases in volume, and begins to feel warm. (It should not feel hot.) You may need to remove it from the heat occasionally to reach the correct thickness and temperature. Do not overcook it or you will curdle the eggs. Spoon the sabayon into decorative glasses. Garnish with a sprig of mint. Serve with ladyfingers and strawberries for dipping.

PINOT NOIR
POACHED PEARS

preparation time · 30 minutes
cooking time · 25–30 minutes
makes · 4 servings

Pears poached in wine are an elegant way to close a special dinner. The pears and sauce can be made a day or two in advance and stored in the refrigerator until needed.

ERIC'S OPTIONS
For Italian-style poached pears, substitute Chianti for the Pinot Noir. Replace the whipped cream with a small dollop of mascarpone cheese.

2 cups	Pinot Noir	500 mL
2 cups	water	500 mL
1 cup	sugar	250 mL
1	cinnamon stick	1
2	whole cloves	2
1 tsp.	vanilla extract	5 mL
4	slightly under-ripe medium-sized pears	4
	whipped cream and mint sprigs	

Combine the Pinot Noir, water, sugar, cinnamon, cloves and vanilla in a pot large enough to hold the pears. Place over medium-high heat and bring to a boil, stirring to dissolve the sugar. Peel and core the pears. (A melon baller works well to core the pear from its blossom end.) Trim a little from the bottom of each pear so it will stand up when served. Add the pears to the syrup. Cover the pan, reduce the heat to medium-low and gently simmer, turning them from time to time. Cook until the pears are just tender, about 15–20 minutes. Remove from the heat and allow to cool in the syrup, turning them over occasionally. Use a slotted spoon to transfer the pears to a plate, standing them up. Store the pears in the fridge until needed.

To make the sauce, boil 1½ cups (375 mL) of the poaching liquid until it is reduced to ½ cup (125 mL). Cool to room temperature and refrigerate until needed. To serve, spoon a little sauce on a dessert plate. Place a pear in the centre and spoon or pipe whipped cream alongside. Garnish with mint.

Leftover poaching liquid can be saved and stored in the fridge for another use. I use it to moisten cake pieces when making trifle or to poach other fruits, such as peaches or apricots.

BLACKBERRY and APPLE PIE

preparation time · 30 minutes
cooking time · 50 minutes
makes · 8 servings

Use your favourite homemade or store-bought crust to make this pie.

ERIC'S OPTIONS
For a sweet and crunchy crust, sprinkle the top of the pie with a little sugar before baking. Slightly under-ripe pears could replace the apples. Raspberries could replace the blackberries.

6	medium apples, peeled, cored and sliced	6
1 Tbsp.	lemon juice	15 mL
2 cups	fresh or frozen (partially thawed) blackberries	500 mL
1/4 cup	granulated sugar	50 mL
1 tsp.	ground cinnamon	5 mL
1/4 tsp.	ground nutmeg	1 mL
2 Tbsp.	all-purpose flour	25 mL
pinch	salt	pinch
1 Tbsp.	butter	15 mL
1	9-inch (23-cm) deep-dish double crust pastry	1
	egg wash (1 large egg beaten with 2 Tbsp./25 mL milk or cream)	

Preheat the oven to 425°F (220°C). Combine the apples, lemon juice, blackberries, sugar, cinnamon, nutmeg, flour and salt in a large bowl and gently toss to combine. Do not overmix or you'll crush the blackberries. Spoon the filling into the bottom pie crust, gently packing it in. Dot the top with butter. Brush the edge of the bottom crust with egg wash. Place the top crust on, crimping the edges to seal. Brush the top of the pie with egg wash. Cut a small hole in the centre of the pie to allow steam to escape. Bake for 20 minutes. Reduce the heat to 325°F (160°C) and cook for 30 minutes more, or until the apples are tender when poked with a thin knife and the filling is bubbling in the centre.

PASTRY for a DOUBLE CRUST PIE

preparation time	·	15 minutes
cooking time	·	none
makes	·	pastry for double crust pie

Handle this pastry delicately and you will be rewarded with a very flaky crust.

3 cups	all-purpose flour	750 mL
1/2 tsp.	salt	2 mL
1 1/4 cups	vegetable shortening	300 mL
1/4 cup	cold butter, cut into small cubes	50 mL
6 Tbsp.	ice-cold water	90 mL

Combine the flour and salt in a bowl. With a pastry cutter or two table knives, cut the shortening and butter into the flour until a pea-sized crumble forms. Pour the water over the dough and gently work it in with a fork or lightly floured hands until it forms into a loose dough that just holds together. Do not overmix or the pastry will be tough. Transfer the dough to a lightly floured work surface and shape into a ball. Cut in half and press each half into a thick disc. Wrap each half in plastic wrap and refrigerate for 15 minutes. Return the dough to the work surface. With a lightly floured rolling pin, roll each disc into a circle large enough to fit the top and bottom of your pie.

STEAMED CRANBERRY and RAISIN PUDDING

preparation time · 30 minutes
cooking time · 1 1/2 – 2 hours
makes · 8 servings

Tart cranberries nicely balance the concentrated sweetness of raisins and currants. Their colour also gives the pudding a festive look, making it a nice alternative to plum pudding at Christmas. Serve wedges of warm pudding with hard sauce, warm custard, ice cream or sweetened whipped cream.

NOTE
Pudding moulds are available at kitchen-ware stores.

ERIC'S OPTIONS
The pudding can be made ahead, unmoulded, cooled, tightly wrapped and stored in the fridge for several days. Reheat for about 5 minutes in the microwave. Steamed pudding can be frozen for up to 2 months. Thaw before reheating.

1	12-oz. (340-g) package fresh or frozen (thawed) cranberries, coarsely chopped	1
1/2 cup	golden raisins	125 mL
1/2 cup	currants	125 mL
1/2 cup	chopped walnuts	125 mL
1 1/2 cups	all-purpose flour	375 mL
1/4 cup	brown sugar, packed	50 mL
1 tsp.	ground cinnamon	5 mL
pinch	ground nutmeg and ground cloves	pinch
1/4 cup	molasses	50 mL
1/4 cup	liquid honey	50 mL
2 tsp.	baking soda	10 mL
1/4 tsp.	salt	1 mL
1/3 cup	boiling water	75 mL

Combine the cranberries, raisins, currants, walnuts, flour, sugar, cinnamon, nutmeg and cloves in a bowl. In another bowl, combine the molasses, honey, baking soda, salt and boiling water, mixing well. Stir the wet mixture into the dry until well combined. The batter will be very thick. Pack into a buttered 6-cup (1.5-L) pudding mould. Cover tightly, ensuring it is watertight, with lightly buttered foil or the pudding mould lid, if it has one. Place on a rack in a large pot. Add boiling water to a depth of 1–2 inches (2.5–5 cm). Cover and steam over medium-high heat, checking the water level occasionally, for 1$^{1/2}$–2 hours, or until the pudding has risen and springs back when lightly touched. [The pudding can also be steamed in a 325°F/160°C oven. Place the covered pudding in a roasting pan. Add boiling water to a depth of 2 inches (5 cm). Tightly cover the roasting pan with a lid or foil and cook for a similar length of time.] When the pudding is cooked, uncover and cool on a rack for 10 minutes before unmoulding on a serving plate.

CHOCOLATE FONDUE
for TWO

preparation time · 15 minutes
cooking time · 5 minutes
makes · 2 servings

A delectable bowl of liquid chocolate designed for two.

ERIC'S OPTIONS
Coffee, hazelnut
or cherry liqueur
can be used
instead of orange
liqueur. Expand
the recipe if you
are entertaining
a larger group.

3/4 cup	whipping cream	175 mL
3 oz.	semisweet chocolate, coarsely chopped	75 g
1 oz.	orange liqueur, such as Grand Marnier	25 mL
	sliced or whole fresh fruit, such as strawberries, kiwi, mango and pineapple	

Place the cream in a small pot. Bring almost to a boil over medium-high heat. Whisk in the chocolate and liqueur, mixing until the chocolate is melted and well incorporated. Remove from the heat and pour into a heatproof bowl or small fondue pot. Arrange the fruit around it. Use small forks or skewers to dip the fruit into the chocolate mixture.

HOT BROWNIE
PUDDING

preparation time · 20 minutes
cooking time · 45–50 minutes
makes · 6 servings

This rich-tasting pudding comes with its own chocolate sauce. Serve it hot or warm with vanilla ice cream, frozen vanilla yogurt or whipped cream.

ERIC'S OPTIONS
The brownie can be made, without the hot water, several hours in advance and stored in the refrigerator. Add the hot water just before baking. Increase the baking time by 5–10 minutes.

1 cup	all-purpose flour	250 mL
3/4 cup	granulated sugar	175 mL
2 tsp.	baking powder	10 mL
1/2 tsp.	salt	2 mL
2 Tbsp.	cocoa powder	25 mL
1/2 cup	milk	125 mL
2 Tbsp.	vegetable oil	25 mL
1 tsp.	vanilla extract	5 mL
3/4 cup	chopped walnuts or pecans	175 mL
3/4 cup	brown sugar	175 mL
4 Tbsp.	cocoa powder	60 mL
1 3/4 cups	hot water	425 mL

Preheat the oven to 350°F (180°C). Sift the flour, granualted sugar, baking powder, salt and 2 Tbsp. (25 mL) of the cocoa into a bowl. Pour in the milk, oil and vanilla and mix until just combined. Mix in the nuts. Spoon and spread the batter, which will be quite thick, into an 8 x 8-inch (20 x 20-cm) baking pan. Mix the brown sugar with the remaining 4 Tbsp. (60 mL) cocoa in a small bowl, then sprinkle it over the batter. Pour the hot water over the mixture. Bake for 45–50 minutes, until the brownie rises to the top and the sauce below is bubbling.

LUSCIOUS LEMON CAKE

preparation time · 20 minutes		
cooking time · 40–45 minutes		
makes · 8 servings		

Here's a moist and delicious cake that lemon lovers will adore.

ERIC'S OPTIONS
This cake, although nice on its own, is even nicer when berry compote is served alongside. Combine sliced or whole fresh or frozen (thawed) berries, such as strawberries, blackberries, blueberries and raspberries, with icing sugar to taste. Mix in 1 Tbsp. (15 mL) chopped fresh mint, if desired. Let the berries stand, covered, for 30 minutes before serving with the cake.

1/2 cup	butter, at room temperature	125 mL
1 1/2 cups	granulated sugar	375 mL
4	large eggs	4
2	lemons, finely grated zest for cake, juice reserved for glaze	2
1 tsp.	vanilla extract	5 mL
2 cups	all-purpose flour	500 mL
2 1/2 tsp.	baking powder	12.5 mL
1/2 tsp.	salt	2 mL
2/3 cup	milk	150 mL
1/2 cup	icing sugar, or to taste	125 mL

Preheat the oven to 350°F (180°C). Lightly grease and flour a 9-inch (23-cm) round cake pan. Beat the butter and sugar until light. Mix in the eggs one at a time. Mix in the lemon zest and vanilla. Sift the flour, baking powder and salt together. Mix the dry ingredients into the wet ingredients alternately with the milk, until just combined. Spoon the batter into the pan. Bake for 40–45 minutes, or until a toothpick inserted into the centre of the cake comes out clean.

Cool the cake on a rack for 30 minutes, and then carefully unmould onto a serving plate. Make a glaze for the cake by combining the lemon juice and icing sugar in a bowl. Brush 1/4 of the glaze on top of the cake. Allow it to soak in, and then brush with 1/4 more glaze. Repeat until all the glaze is used.

CREAMY COFFEE CHEESECAKE

preparation time · 20 minutes
cooking time · 50–60 minutes
makes · 8 servings

A rich and creamy cake with a caffeine kick.

THE CRUST	1 1/4 cups	graham cracker or cookie crumbs	300 mL
	1/3 cup	melted butter	75 mL
	1/4 cup	sugar	50 mL
	2 Tbsp.	cocoa	25 mL
THE FILLING	3	9-oz. (250-g) packages cream cheese	3
	1 cup	sugar	250 mL
	3	large eggs	3
	1 Tbsp.	instant coffee granules	15 mL
	2 Tbsp.	boiling water	25 mL
	1 tsp.	vanilla extract	5 mL

THE CRUST

Preheat the oven to 300°F (150°C). Combine the crust ingredients and press into the bottom and partially up the sides of a 10-inch (25-cm) springform cake pan.

THE FILLING

Beat the cream cheese until smooth. Gradually beat in the sugar. Beat in the eggs one at a time, scraping the sides of the bowl after each addition. Combine the coffee with the boiling water and mix to dissolve. Beat it and the vanilla into the cream cheese mixture. Pour the batter into the crust. To help prevent cheesecake from cracking, place a pan of water in the bottom of the oven during baking. Bake for 50–60 minutes, or until the centre of the cake barely jiggles when the pan is tapped. Place the cake on a rack and cool to room temperature. To prevent cracking after baking, run a sharp, wet knife around the edge of the cake to a depth of 1 inch (2.5 cm) before refrigerating. Refrigerate for at least 3 hours before unmoulding and serving.

INDEX

Almond Cranberry Biscotti, 162

Annette's Swedish Pepparkakor, 164

Antipasto, Roasted Pepper on Parmesan Toasts, 12

Appetizer menu planning, 3

Apple and Blackberry Pie, 172

Asparagus

    Asparagus, Roasted Pepper and Mushroom Strudel, 80

    Balsamic Roasted Asparagus, 146

    Stuffed Baked Potatoes with Aged Cheddar and
      Asparagus, 82

Baked Chilled Salmon Fillets with Dill and Horseradish
    Sauce, 62

Baked Snapper with Hoisin Sesame Glaze, 71

Balsamic Roasted Asparagus, 146

Beans

    Oak Bay Baked Beans, 136

    Yam Salad with Red Onions, Black Beans and
      Cilantro, 28

Beef

    Beef and Macaroni Casserole, 56

    Cheryl's Beef and Potato Moussaka, 118

    Chunky Chili with Dark Ale, 122

    Eric's Tourtière, 126

    Glazed Meatloaf with Onion Gravy, 120

    Grandma Akis's Hamburger Steaks, 116

    Greek-Style Mini Burgers on Cucumber Rounds, 5

    Grilled Sirloin on Rice Noodles with Green Onions,
      Garlic and Ginger, 58

    New York Steak Crostini with Gremolata
      Mayonnaise, 9

    Pot Roast Braised with Port and Rosemary, 124

    Southern-Style Short Ribs, 114

    Veal-Stuffed Pasta Shells with Olive Tomato Sauce, 54

Beer and Chili Steamed Mussels, 73

Beets, Chilled Soup, 43

Biscotti, Almond Cranberry, 162

Biscuits, Blue Cheese, 141

Blackberry and Apple Pie, 172

Blanching vegetables, 83

Blue Cheese Biscuits, 141

Bouillabaisse, Canadian-Style, 72

Bow-Tie Pasta with Kale, Anchovies and Parmesan, 48

Braising and stewing meat, 129

Brandy-Laced Peppercorn Pâté on Baguette Rounds, 10

Brussels Sprouts Stir-Fried with Red Onions and
    Peppers, 150

Butter Cookies, Devie's Maple Pecan, 160

Buttermilk Yukon Gold Mashed Potatoes, 151

Cabbage

    Cabbage Soup with Smoked Turkey and Rosemary, 42

    Southern-Spiced Coleslaw with Jicama and Corn, 27

Caesar Salad, Light and Delicious, 20

Cake, Luscious Lemon, 178

Canadian-Style Bouillabaisse, 72

Caramelized Onion and Stilton Tarts, 16

Carrot, Garlic and Chive Soup, 32

Carrots

    Carrot, Garlic and Chive Soup, 32

    Carrots with Honey, Ginger and Lemon, 147

    Moroccan-Spiced Potato and Carrot Salad, 29

Cauliflower Soup with Curry and Coconut Milk, 37

Cedar Plank Salmon, 66

Champagne Sabayon, 170

Cheese

    Beef and Macaroni Casserole, 56

    Blue Cheese Biscuits, 141

    Caramelized Onion and Stilton Tarts, 16

    Creole-Style Stuffed Eggplant, 85

    Monterey Jack and Jalapeño Cornbread, 140

    Organic Greens with Pears, Pecans and
      Crumbled Stilton, 18

    Port-Marinated Strawberries Wrapped in Prosciutto, 2

    Quick and Easy Chicken Enchiladas, 103

    Roasted Vegetable Lasagna with Ricotta Filling, 52

    Romaine with Oranges, Feta and Olives, 19

    Stuffed Baked Potatoes with Aged Cheddar and
      Asparagus, 82

    Tomato and Goat Cheese Salad, 25

    Veal-Stuffed Pasta Shells with Olive Tomato Sauce, 54

    Zucchini Rounds with Cambozola and Cherry Tomatoes, 4

Cheesecake, Creamy Coffee, 179
Cheryl's Beef and Potato Moussaka, 118
Chewy Oatmeal Cranberry Cookies, 154
Chicken
    Brandy-Laced Peppercorn Pâté on Baguette
        Rounds, 10
    Chicken Wings with Heat, Honey and Rum, 6
    Cornmeal-Crusted Chicken Legs, 98
    Fettuccini with Chicken, Pesto and Cherry
        Tomatoes, 49
    Garlic-Stuffed Chicken Legs with Pan Gravy, 99
    Grilled Chicken with Summer Berries and Goat
        Cheese, 96
    Honey and Citrus-Glazed Chicken Breast, 97
    Japanese-Style Chicken Skewers with Ginger
        Sauce, 7
    One-Pan Mediterranean-Style Chicken Dinner, 102
    Quick and Easy Chicken Enchiladas, 103
    Roast Chicken Scented with Lemon, Garlic and
        Rosemary, 92
    Spinach and Raisin-Stuffed Chicken Breasts, 94
    Teriyaki Chicken and Vegetable Stir-Fry, 100
Chili, Chunky with Dark Ale, 122
Chilled Beet Soup, 43
Chipotle peppers, about, 135
Chocolate
    Chewy Oatmeal Cranberry Cookies, 154
    Chocolate Lover's Cookies, 161
    Chocolate Macadamia Nut Shortbread, 159
    Fondue for Two, 176
    Hot Brownie Pudding, 177
    Meringue Kisses, 165
    Pantry Cookies, 158
Chunky Chili with Dark Ale, 122
Cold Strawberry Soup with Mint and Black Pepper, 44
Coleslaw, Southern-Spiced, with Jicama and Corn, 27
Corn, Creamy Soup, 36
Cornbread, Monterey Jack and Jalapeño, 140
Cornish Game Hens
    Sage and Mustard-Crusted, 104
    With Orange, Rosemary and Cranberry Glaze, 105
Cornmeal-Crusted Chicken Legs, 98
Crab
    Cornmeal-Crusted Crab Cakes with Cayenne
        Mayonnaise, 74
    Pork and Crab Pot Stickers, 14

Creamy Coffee Cheesecake, 179
Creamy Corn Soup, 36
Creole-Style Stuffed Eggplant, 85
Cucumber Rounds with Greek-Style Mini Burgers, 5
Curry
    Cauliflower Soup with Curry and Coconut Milk, 37
    Curried Vegetable Stew, 90

Devie's Maple Pecan Butter Cookies, 160
Duck
    Brandy-Laced Peppercorn Pâté on Baguette Rounds, 10
    Spice-Roasted Duck with Hoisin Glaze, 110

Eggplant, Creole-Style Stuffed, 85
Enchiladas, Quick and Easy Chicken, 103
Eric's Tourtière, 126
Exotic Mushroom Risotto, 86

Fettuccini with Chicken, Pesto and Cherry
    Tomatoes, 49
Filo Pastry
    About, 81
    Asparagus, Roasted Pepper and Mushroom
        Strudel, 80
    Halibut and Spinach Wrapped in Filo, 64
Fish and Fresh Vegetable Casserole, 70
Fish and shellfish, buying and storing, 61
Fish, baking, 63
Five-Onion Soup, 38
Fondue for Two, Chocolate, 176

Garlic-Stuffed Chicken Legs with Pan Gravy, 99
Glazed Meatloaf with Onion Gravy, 120
Glazed Yams with Cranberries and Pecans, 148
Grandma Akis's Hamburger Steaks, 116
Gravy
    Chicken, 92, 99
    Onion Gravy for Glazed Meatloaf, 120
Greek-Style Mini Burgers on Cucumber Rounds, 5
Gremolata Mayonnaise on New York Steak Crostini, 9
Grilled Chicken with Summer Berries and Goat
    Cheese, 96
Grilled Prawns on Sweet, Sour and Spicy Mangoes, 76
Grilled Sirloin on Rice Noodles with Green Onions,
    Garlic and Ginger, 58

Halibut
    Fish and Fresh Vegetable Casserole, 70
    Halibut and Spinach Wrapped in Filo, 64
Heavenly Spiced Turkey and Vegetable Kebabs, 108
Herbs, substituting dried for fresh, 131
Honey and Citrus-Glazed Chicken Breast, 97
Hot Brownie Pudding, 177
Hot-Smoked Salmon on Mini New Potatoes, 8

Japanese-Style Chicken Skewers with Ginger Sauce, 7
Jicama
    About, 27
    Southern-Spiced Coleslaw with Jicama and Corn, 27

Kale with Bow-Tie Pasta, Anchovies and
    Parmesan, 48
Kebabs, Heavenly Spiced Turkey and Vegetable, 108

Lamb
    Greek-Style Mini Burgers on Cucumber Rounds, 5
    Lamb Chops with Blackcurrant Sauce, 130
    Lamb Shanks Braised with Tomatoes, Rosemary
        and Garlic, 128
    Lemony Lamb Chops with Artichokes, Olives
        and Mint, 132
Lasagna, Roasted Vegetable with Ricotta Filling, 52
Lemon Cake, Luscious, 178
Lemony Lamb Chops with Artichokes, Olives and
    Mint, 132
Lettuce, preparing for salads, 21
Light and Delicious Caesar Salad, 20
Luscious Lemon Cake, 178

Mangoes, Sweet, Sour and Spicy with Grilled
    Prawns, 76
Maple Whiskey-Glazed Salmon, 60
Measuring ingredients, 155
Meat, braising and stewing, 129
Meatloaf, Glazed, with Onion Gravy, 120
Meringue Kisses, 165
Monterey Jack and Jalapeño Cornbread, 140
Moroccan-Spiced Potato and Carrot Salad, 29
Moussaka, Cheryl's Beef and Potato, 118
Mushrooms
    Exotic Mushroom Risotto, 86
    Grandma Akis's Hamburger Steaks, 116

Mushrooms (continued)
    Portobello Mushroom Burgers with Lemon Basil
        Mayonnaise, 84
Mussels, Beer and Chili Steamed, 73

New York Steak Crostini with Gremolata
    Mayonnaise, 9
Nuts, purchasing and storing, 155

Oak Bay Baked Beans, 136
Oatmeal Cookies with Cranberries, 154
One-Pan Mediterranean-Style Chicken Dinner, 102
Onions
    Caramelized Onion and Stilton Tarts, 16
    Five-Onion Soup, 38
Oranges with Romaine, Feta and Olives, 19
Organic Greens with Pears, Pecans and Crumbled
    Stilton, 18
Orzo Baked with Green Onions and Parmesan, 145

Pan-Seared Pork Cutlets with Grainy Mustard Sauce, 138
Pantry Cookies, 158
Pasta
    Beef and Macaroni Casserole, 56
    Bow-Tie Pasta with Kale, Anchovies and
        Parmesan, 48
    Fettuccini with Chicken, Pesto and Cherry
        Tomatoes, 49
    Orzo Baked with Green Onions and Parmesan, 145
    Preparing, 47
    Rigatoni with Italian Sausage, Peppers and Feta, 46
    Roasted Vegetable Lasagna with Ricotta Filling, 52
    Spinach Tortellini with Creamy Lemon and Leek
        Sauce, 51
    Tomato, Prosciutto and Garlic-Steamed Clams on
        Linguini, 50
    Tortellini Soup with Italian Sausage and Crumbled
        Feta, 39
    Veal-Stuffed Pasta Shells with Olive Tomato Sauce, 54
Pastry for a Double Crust Pie, 173
Pâté, Brandy-Laced Peppercorn, on Baguette
    Rounds, 10
Pears
    Organic Greens with Pears, Pecans and Crumbled
        Stilton, 18
    Pinot Noir Poached, 171

Peppers
    Asparagus, Roasted Pepper and Mushroom Strudel, 80
    Chipotle, about, 135
    Roasted Pepper and Spinach Salad, 24
    Roasted Pepper Antipasto on Parmesan Toasts, 12
    Roasting, 13
Pie
    Blackberry and Apple, 172
    Pastry for a Double Crust Pie, 173
Pineapple, Fresh Rum-Glazed, 168
Pinot Noir Poached Pears, 171
Planning an appetizer menu, 3
Plum Tomato, Onion and Caper Salad, 26
Pork
    Chunky Chili with Dark Ale, 122
    Eric's Tourtière, 126
    Glazed Meatloaf with Onion Gravy, 120
    Oak Bay Baked Beans, 136
    Pan-Seared Pork Cutlets with Grainy Mustard
       Sauce, 138
    Pork and Crab Pot Stickers, 14
    Pork Side Ribs with Chipotle Barbecue Sauce, 134
    Prosciutto-Wrapped Pork Loin with Salsa Verde, 133
Port-Marinated Strawberries Wrapped in Prosciutto, 2
Portobello Mushroom Burgers with Lemon Basil
    Mayonnaise, 84
Potatoes
    Buttermilk Yukon Gold Mashed Potatoes, 151
    Cheryl's Beef and Potato Moussaka, 118
    Hot-Smoked Salmon on Mini New Potatoes, 8
    Moroccan-Spiced Potato and Carrot Salad, 29
    Roasted New Potatoes with Lemon and Dijon, 152
    Stuffed Baked Potatoes with Aged Cheddar and
       Asparagus, 82
Pot Roast Braised with Port and Rosemary, 124
Pot Stickers, Pork and Crab, 14
Prawns
    Fettuccini with Chicken or Prawns, Pesto and Cherry
       Tomatoes, 49
    Grilled Prawns on Sweet, Sour and Spicy Mangoes, 76
    Prawn Bisque, 40
    Prawns and shrimp, about, 77
Prosciutto-Wrapped Pork Loin with Salsa Verde, 133
Pudding
    Hot Brownie Pudding, 177
    Steamed Cranberry and Raisin Pudding, 174

Quick and Easy Chicken Enchiladas, 103
Quick Rouille, 143

Ribs, Southern-Style Short, 114
Rice
    About risotto, 86
    Exotic Mushroom Risotto, 86
Rice Noodles with Grilled Sirloin, Green Onions,
    Garlic and Ginger, 58
Rigatoni with Italian Sausage, Peppers and Feta, 46
Risotto, Exotic Mushroom, 86
Roast Chicken Scented with Lemon, Garlic and
    Rosemary, 92
Roasted New Potatoes with Lemon and Dijon, 152
Roasted Pepper and Spinach Salad, 24
Roasted Pepper Antipasto on Parmesan Toasts, 12
Roasted Vegetable Lasagna with Ricotta Filling, 52
Romaine with Oranges, Feta and Olives, 19
Rouille, Quick, 143
Rum-Glazed Fresh Pineapple Rings, 168

Sabayon, Champagne, 170
Sage and Mustard Crusted Cornish Game Hen, 104
Salad dressing, preparing, 23
Salmon
    Baked Chilled Salmon Fillets with Dill and Horseradish
       Sauce, 62
    Cedar Plank Salmon, 66
    Fish and Fresh Vegetable Casserole, 70
    Hot-Smoked Salmon on Mini New Potatoes, 8
    Maple Whiskey-Glazed Salmon, 60
Salsa
    Salsa Verde, 133
    Speedy, 142
    Tortilla Chips with Shrimp and Corn Salsa, 3
Sauces
    Quick Rouille, 143
    Tzatziki, 144
Sausages in Tortellini Soup with Crumbled Feta, 39
Shepherd's Pie, Turkey with Yukon Gold Mashed
    Potatoes, 106
Shortbread
    Chocolate Macadamia Nut, 159
    Whipped, 156
Shrimp
    Shrimp and prawns, about, 77

Shrimp (continued)
    Shrimp-Stuffed Sole Fillets, 68
    Tropical Shrimp Salad, 30
Snapper
    Baked Snapper with Hoisin Sesame Glaze, 71
    Fish and Fresh Vegetable Casserole, 70
Sole Fillets, Shrimp-Stuffed, 68
Soup, freezing, 35
Soup stock, making, 33
Southern-Spiced Coleslaw with Jicama and Corn, 27
Southern-Style Short Ribs, 114
Speedy Salsa, 142
Spice-Roasted Duck with Hoisin Glaze, 110
Spinach
    Roasted Pepper and Spinach Salad, 24
    Spinach and Raisin-Stuffed Chicken Breasts, 94
    Spinach Tortellini with Creamy Lemon and Leek
      Sauce, 51
    Spring Vegetable Salad, 22
Spring Vegetable Salad, 22
Steamed Cranberry and Raisin Pudding, 174
Stew, Curried Vegetable, 90
Stewing and braising meat, 129
Stir-Fries
    Brussels Sprouts Stir-Fried with Red Onions and
      Peppers, 150
    How to stir-fry, 101
    Teriyaki Chicken and Vegetable Stir-Fry, 100
Strawberries
    Cold Strawberry Soup with Mint and Black
      Pepper, 44
    Port-Marinated Strawberries Wrapped in
      Prosciutto, 2
    Strawberries in Sparkling Wine with Honey Whipped
      Cream, 169
Strudel with Asparagus, Roasted Pepper and
    Mushroom, 80
Stuffed Baked Potatoes with Aged Cheddar and
    Asparagus, 82

Summer Harvest Soup, 34
Sweet potatoes, about, 149

Tarts, Caramelized Onion and Stilton, 16
Teriyaki Chicken and Vegetable Stir-Fry, 100
Tomatoes
    Plum Tomato, Onion and Caper Salad, 26
    Tomato and Goat Cheese Salad, 25
    Tomato, Prosciutto and Garlic- Steamed Clams on
      Linguini, 50
Tortellini Soup with Italian Sausage and Crumbled
    Feta, 39
Tortilla Chips with Shrimp and Corn Salsa, 3
Tourtière
    Eric's (meat), 126
    Vegetarian, 88
Tropical Shrimp Salad, 30
Tuna Steaks Roasted with Basil, Wine and Capers, 67
Turkey
    Cabbage Soup with Smoked Turkey and Rosemary, 42
    Glazed Meatloaf with Onion Gravy, 120
    Heavenly Spiced Turkey and Vegetable Kebabs, 108
    Shepherd's Pie with Yukon Gold Mashed Potatoes, 106
Tzatziki Sauce, 144

Veal-Stuffed Pasta Shells with Olive Tomato Sauce, 54
Vegetables, blanching, 83
Vegetarian Tourtière, 88

Whipped Shortbread, 156

Yams
    About, 149
    Glazed Yams with Cranberries and Pecans, 148
    Yam Salad with Red Onions, Black Beans and
      Cilantro, 28

Zucchini Rounds with Cambozola and Cherry Tomatoes, 4